Free Yourself From Student Loan Debt

Get Out from Under Once and for All

Brian O'Connell

Dearborn™
Trade Publishing
A **Kaplan Professional** Company

This publication is designed to provide accurate and authoritative information in regard to the subject matter covered. It is sold with the understanding that the publisher is not engaged in rendering legal, accounting, or other professional service. If legal advice or other expert assistance is required, the services of a competent professional person should be sought.

Vice President and Publisher: Cynthia A. Zigmund
Acquisitions Editor: Mary B. Good
Senior Managing Editor: Jack Kiburz
Interior Design: Lucy Jenkins
Cover Design: DePinto Studios
Typesetting: Elizabeth Pitts

Published by Dearborn Trade Publishing
A Kaplan Professional Company

Printed in the United States of America

04 05 06 10 9 8 7 6 5 4 3 2 1

Library of Congress Cataloging-in-Publication Data

O'Connell, Brian, 1959–
    Free yourself from student loan debt : get out from under once and for all / by Brian O'Connell.
        p. cm.
    Includes index.
    ISBN 0-7931-8795-8 (pbk.)
1. Student loan funds—United States. 2. College graduates—United States—Finance, Personal. I. Title.
    LB2340.2.O36   2004
    378.3′62—dc22

                                                                    2004001492

Dearborn Trade books are available at special quantity discounts to use for sales promotions, employee premiums, or educational purposes. Please call our Special Sales Department to order or for more information at 800-245-2665, e-mail trade@dearborn.com, or write to Dearborn Trade Publishing, 30 South Wacker Drive, Suite 2500, Chicago, IL 60606-7481.

DEDICATION

This book is dedicated to my three children, Madison, Cooper, and Chip. All are going to college someday, and all will face the same financial challenges that you and I did. The real challenge is to make sure they read this book before they go.

A c k n o w l e d g m e n t s

I want to thank my agent, Stacey Glick, for steering this book my way; and I want to thank my editor, Mary Good, who, I found, has the patience of a saint when it comes to writers and deadlines.

Some debt is good. Consider the farmer's attitude toward natural fertilizer. Using it may be an assault on the olfactory senses, but you can't argue with the results.

The same goes for your college debts. Student loan debt isn't bad debt, it's good debt. Think of it as a down payment for your future—that's the mind-set you're looking for. After all, studies show that in addition to the inherent benefits of a higher education, a college degree is worth 75 percent more than a high school diploma or more than $1,000,000 over a lifetime in the workforce.

But it's still debt. And you have to pay it off. And brother, do Americans have a lot of student debt to pay off. Here's a look at the facts:

- The average American college student owes about $15,000 in loans after graduation. Quadruple that amount if you're the average grad school graduate.
- According to the Washington, D.C.–based State's PIRG Higher Education Project, 39 percent of student borrowers now graduate with unmanageable levels of debt, meaning that their monthly payments are more than 8 percent of their monthly incomes.
- According to data from the U.S. Department of Education's National Postsecondary Student Aid Study (NPSAS), not only are the majority of students turning to loans to finance college, but debt levels are also escalating. In 1999–2000, 64 percent of students graduated with student loan debt, and

the average student loan debt has nearly doubled over the past eight years to $16,928.

- In 1999–2000, 71 percent of students from families with incomes less than $20,000 graduated with debt, compared to 44 percent of students from families with incomes more than $100,000.
- Approximately 55 percent of African-American student borrowers and 58 percent of Hispanic student borrowers graduated with unmanageable debt burden.

THE ART OF DIGGING OUT

Okay, so the amount of student loan debt facing young Americans is pervasive, if not problematic. So what's to be done about it? Find creative ways to pay off student debt, that's what.

In this book, *Free Yourself from Student Loan Debt,* I'll demonstrate the best ways to rid yourself of student loan debt—fast and as relatively painless as possible.

I'll show you the insider's guide to handling student loan debt. From identifying the amount of student loan debt you have (and who holds the loan) to understanding the different forms of payment options, *Free Yourself from Student Loan Debt* will guide you through the student loan maze and out into the rarified air of the debt-free career professional.

Inside these pages I'll demonstrate how you can:

- Convince financial institutions to "forgive" your loans.
- Find out what happens when you don't pay your loan—and how you can fix the problem with no lasting impact on your credit and finances.
- "Consolidate" your loan for easier (and lower) payments.
- Defer your loans with no penalty.
- Take a "break" from your student loans through a mechanism called "forbearance."

- Realize that only six minimum payments can get you out of default status.
- Take creative steps when you can't pay your student loans.
- Fight the government and financial institutions who claim you didn't pay your student loan debt years after you did.
- Pay off your loans and invest for your future at the same time.

And that's just the tip of the iceberg.

In researching *Free Yourself from Student Loan Debt* I've talked to dozens of experts, from loan managers to student loan advocates, to assess the best way of getting out of student loan debt. I'll roll out real-life case studies and anecdotes about how savvy students got out of debt using often overlooked but perfectly legitimate loan management techniques. I'll back up everything with easy-to-understand *USA Today*–type infoboxes, sidebars, and colorful industry profiles, and package it together in one lively, user-friendly book. As a bonus, I'll offer 50-plus surefire tips to eliminating student loan debt.

After finishing *Free Yourself from Student Loan Debt,* you'll have the tools and knowledge to radically change the way you look at student loan debt, and to view loan management in revolutionary new ways.

More important, you will possess the tools you need to pay off that student loan debt quickly, affordably, and permanently.

Brian O'Connell
Winter, 2004

Brian O'Connell is a former Wall Street bond trader turned business writer. He is the author of eight popular books, including *CNBC Creating Wealth, The 401(k) Millionaire,* and *Investing in Separate Accounts.* He also contributes articles to a variety of publications, including the *Wall Street Journal, Newsweek, USA Today,* and *Bloomberg Wealth Advisor.* When not writing, he appears on local, regional, and national television and radio programs discussing financial and investing topics.

O'Connell resides in Bucks County, Pennsylvania, and can be reached by e-mail at brian.oco@verizon.net.

1

GETTING ORGANIZED

Woody Allen once said that when it comes to your financial situation, money is better than poverty, if only for financial reasons. This is a good line, and one that is completely appropriate for the mind-set of the student loan borrower. You know, the one who borrowed all that money to march off to college and study Shakespeare and shoot dice. The one who learned the Pythagorean theorem and how to pour the perfect mug of beer. In other words, you.

Yes, you.

Now that you've done the boolah-boolah, raccoon-coat thing and earned your sheepskin, it's time to face the music, pay the piper, or any other inane cliché you can think of and pay off that college debt. And fast.

The good news is that you're not alone. According to Heather Boushey, an economist at the U.S. Center for Economic and Policy Research, student loan debt is 85 percent higher for students in 2003 than it was for students who borrowed money in 1993. In her March 2003 paper, "The Debt Explosion among College

Graduates," Boushey reports that 1999–2000 college graduates owe more than their predecessors ever did. The numbers tell the story:

- On average, college graduates in 1999–2000 owed $15,000 in student loan debt compared to $8,200 for students who graduated in 1989–1990.
- Those figures rise when private, four-year college graduates are taken into account. Those graduates owed $16,500 on average in 1999–2000 compared to $10,600 in 1989-1990.
- Two out of three (67.9 percent) of college graduates in 1999–2000 borrowed money for college, up from less than half (46.3 percent) in 1992–1993.

THE COLD, HARSH REALITY OF STUDENT LOAN DEBT

The ramifications of all that debt are not pretty. By and large, there's no getting around the fact that you *have* to pay off your student loans. Such loans are rarely granted default status and none are ever abolished in bankruptcy situations. Then there is the credit report issue. If you don't pay off your loan, that can haunt you the rest of your life in the form of a bad credit report. And a bad credit report means no new car, no new home, and virtually no hope of ever borrowing money from creditors again. Think Hester Prynne in *The Scarlet Letter* and you get the idea. The only difference is that instead of that scarlet letter *A* for adultery that Prynne bore, you'll be wearing a metaphorical letter *D* for deadbeat until you can pay off your debt.

Besides, ignoring your college debts won't make them go away. Instead, that will just make things worse. If you take the ostrich route and stick your head in the sand every time a loan statement arrives in the mail, you're just staving off the inevitable. By not paying, or delaying, substantial costs—in the form of interest and penalties—could very well be added to your college loan bill.

Translated: Student loans are serious business. That's why knowing the particulars of your student loan—account terms, timetables for payment, penalties, for example—is so crucial. Consequently, facing up to the significant responsibilities stemming from your student loan is the first step in paying them off.

The next step in freeing yourself from student loan debt is to craft a master plan or blueprint to work from as you pay off your loan. After all, you can't manage your student loan debt unless you can manage your overall personal finances.

But to control your student loan debt, as in most other instances, you have to walk before you can run. That's why knowing the financial basics—the terms of your debt, how to craft a household budget, the machinations behind credit and debt, and the importance of eliminating "bad" debt—is so important to your student loan situation.

So, in the spirit of that "Walk first, run second" mantra I've been prattling away about, it's imperative that you have your everyday financial life in order. Here's where to start.

L o a n S n a p s h o t

KNOWLEDGE IS GOOD

Studies show that a college degree is worth 75 percent more than a high school diploma or more than $1,000,000 over a lifetime in the workforce.

KNOW YOUR DEBT

Some people treat student debt like the plague and make no special effort to pay bills right away or at all. The good news is that the number of those who elect to ignore their student loan debt is declining. According to the U.S. Department of Education, student loan default rates have dropped from 22 percent in 1990 to 5.9 percent in 2001. Educators attribute that decline to an improved U.S. economy in the 1990s and an improved awareness on the part of loan recipients of the importance of paying off their student loan debts.

Obviously, student loan borrowers are taking their debt more seriously. And people are beginning to understand that knowledge is power and that the fastest way to pay off student loans is for borrowers to face their loans head on and know what they're up against.

This is a highly significant occurrence. By knowing your debt and understanding how it impacts your financial life, your chances of eliminating that fiscal albatross around your neck increases exponentially. But what, exactly, does "knowing your debt" mean?

For starters, it means knowing how much you owe on your loan. If you owe $8,000, then, if nothing else, you know where you stand. It seems like a simple concept, but some people can't be bothered about their debt amounts. They're too busy starting their careers or tackling other, more appealing, fiscal responsibilities such as buying a new Jeep or grabbing a vacation rental on the beach for the summer. These people are in the highest danger of defaulting on their student loans, simply because, for whatever reason, they stopped paying attention to their loans.

Don't be like that. Know your loan. Know its terms, its payment schedules, its repayment options. Know that if you make higher monthly payments you can pay the loan off more quickly. Know who your lender is and where you can reach them. Know that if you move, you need to contact your lender and let them know your new address. Hey, young people move all the time. They get jobs in different cities or decide that they want to live in San Francisco or Boston at least one time in their lives and up and do so.

Knowing your debt also means knowing what to do if you can't make a monthly payment for some reason. Lenders are usually fairly gracious about this, as long as you let them know you won't be paying and when they can expect the next payment.

Keeping your lender in the loop is a huge part of knowing your debt. Closing them out or ignoring them will only lead to complications and possibly default. And if that happens, good luck landing that new brownstone apartment in Haight-Asbury or Harvard Square.

Above all, knowing your debt means reading and understanding all the correspondence you'll receive from your lending institution. Yes, the language lenders use in their statements reads like the *Dead Sea Scrolls*. But read it anyway. Remember that it's all part of knowing your debt.

And knowing your debt could mean the difference between financial freedom down the road or financial fiasco.

L o a n   S n a p s h o t

IF YOU GOT THE MONEY, HONEY, I GOT THE TIME

When the cost of attending a good four-year college rivals the cost of a good four-bedroom colonial in the burbs, you know sticker shock isn't too far away. According to the College Board in its 2003 report "Trends in College Pricing Survey," tuition and fees at four-year public colleges rose an average of 14.1 percent from 2002–2003.

For the current academic year 2003, tuition at public colleges averaged $4,694, up almost $600 from the year before.

THOSE CREDIT CARD BLUES

Not all debts are bad ones. Using a mortgage to buy a home, tackling the rising costs of college with a loan, even borrowing money to buy a car—all are good debts with high return values.

But there are bad debts, too, debts that can limit or even prohibit your cleaning up your student loan debt. Of the bad debts, few are worse than credit card debt.

Simply stated, credit card debt can kill you from a personal finance point of view. Massive credit card debt can choke your ability to deal with all your other financial responsibilities, taking over your life and limiting your ability to grow and prosper.

Sure, eating at a five-star restaurant or buying season tickets to watch the Red Sox are worthwhile pursuits—if you can afford them with what you bring home in your wallet every payday. Using a credit card to finance these endeavors is being a long-term loser, if only because most of the things you buy with credit cards depreciate rather than rise in value. Those high-top Reebok basketball sneakers may look great in the box, but once you slap them on your feet, their value resides only in your mind's eye, because few others want them anymore. Unlike other depreciable items, like a car that provides vital transportation or a pair of eyeglasses that allows you to see, most things you buy with a credit card don't offer much to your personal bottom line.

From your student loan perspective, any money that is earmarked toward your credit card debt is money that you can't use to free yourself from student loan debt. That's the primary reason why credit card debt is invariably bad debt.

It's bad from a student loan point of view, as well. In fact, student loan debt and credit card debt are joined at the hip. For decades, credit card companies have targeted college students, offering them their first shiny new plastic card while downplaying the dark side of owning a credit card.

Well, that plan worked. Millions of young Americans who received their first credit cards in college (and millions more who didn't, but got them right after they graduated and obtained their first job) have developed the nasty habit of using their credit cards with alarming regularity. In the process, younger Americans have put a real dent in their financial health and made it even harder to address their student loan debts.

According to the college-lending agency Nellie Mae, U.S. college students in 2000 racked up an average credit card balance of $2,748. That's up from an average $1,879 in 1998, the agency reports. More disturbingly, Nellie Mae also says that a college student who makes the *bare minimum* credit card monthly payment (with an 18 percent APR interest rate) would need a whopping 15 years to pay off that entire debt. Worse, the cardholder would have to pay as much in interest alone as he or she would the original $2,748 debt. And that's operating with the dubious assumption that the cardholder would *never use the card again*.

As if, right?

Then there's another study published by New York State's education agency that reports 78 percent of college students carried at least one credit card while 32 percent carried four cards or more. Furthermore, 10 percent of students shouldered a credit card balance of $7,000. Another 14 percent owed between $3,000 and $7,000.

L o a n   S n a p s h o t

DIGGIN' THEM HOLES, AH-AH

According to the U.S. Department of Education's National Postsecondary Student Aid Study (NPSAS), 39 percent of student borrowers now graduate with unmanageable levels of debt. That means their monthly payments are more than 8 percent of their monthly incomes.

Remember what I said at the opening of this chapter? About how the average student loan debt had reached $15,000? Now how in the name of Ivana Trump can someone who already owes $15,000 in student loan debt pay that debt off when they have a $7,000 credit card debt? Answer: In almost all cases, they can't.

BREAKING THE CREDIT CARD CYCLE

That's why managing your personal finances—especially your credit card debt—is job one when it comes to squaring your student loan debt. While credit cards are a necessary evil, when you're trying to free yourself from student loan debt, they can be more evil than necessary. How so? Well, try paying off your college loans when your monthly Visa statement looks like the annual operating budget for Portugal. In many cases, the interest rate on credit cards is 16 percent or more; the interest you pay is not tax-deductible; and quite often the money you owe is for something you've already gotten the most use out of. Pay it off.

But first, make sure the credit card bill is accurate. Analyze the bill. Make sure it matches your receipts. Sometimes when you sign on the dotted line, you don't double-check the amount of the purchase. For example, amid the rush of holiday shopping, you might not have been charged the sale price for an item; you might have been charged twice for a single item; or you could even have been charged for an item purchased by someone else in line. It happens. If you notice a discrepancy, call your credit card issuer and dispute the charge.

Meanwhile, don't fall for any season's greetings from your credit card company offering to lower your minimum payment or saying that because you're such a good customer, you can skip this month's payment. That sounds enticing, but remember, the interest rate clock is still ticking.

With all your holiday shopping, in addition to your regular expenses, suppose that your January credit card bill is $2,500, a typical amount. If the annual interest rate is 18 percent, skipping January's payment could cost you about $38 in finance charges that will show up in next month's bill. No wonder the credit card company is so nice.

HELP YOURSELF, HELP YOUR COUNTRY

As I said, all debts are not bad. In fact, your student loan debt, while tough to pay off, is very good debt. Not only is it good for you, but it's good for your country.

Here is what I mean:

- The U.S. Department of Education reports that every $1 invested in federal financial aid produces $3 for the U.S. Treasury in tax revenue.
- The U.S. Department of Labor reports that according to the Bureau of Labor Statistics, 60 percent of new jobs created through 2010 will require a higher education.
- According to the Institute for Higher Education Policy, your college degree means a lot not just to yourself, but to your country. A college graduate means more tax revenue, greater productivity, increased consumer consumption, decreased reliance on government financial assistance, and expanded workforce flexibility.
- The Advisory Committee on Student Financial Assistance estimates that getting more of America's youth involved in higher education could add $250 billion to the gross domestic product and $80 billion in tax revenues to the U.S. Treasury.

BUILDING A BUDGET

Irish humorist Joseph O'Connor once said, "I feel these days like a very large flamingo. No matter which way I turn, I have this large bill attached to me." While O'Connor aptly states the emotional condition of the high-debt sufferer, there's no need to flap your wings over a big student loan bill. No need, that is, if you know how to control your debt.

The idea here is simple. Control your debt by managing your lifestyle. Consequently, the key to controlling debt is to first try to live as inexpensively as possible. If that means renting an apartment with a roommate or bringing a bag lunch, then so much the better. Once you pay off your student loans you can ramp up your lifestyle, because you'll have more cash at your disposal.

Let's start with a household budget. Without going through the punishing ordeal of ranking your spending priorities, it is difficult to guarantee you will have anything left over at the end of the month to pay your student loan. If this sounds too taxing, then use the paperless budget method. Start by holding out a reasonable portion of every paycheck to pay down your student loan and other debts and force yourself to live on the balance.

If every now and then you come out ahead, be sure to apply your windfall to eliminate student loan debts before you start to accumulate savings. This makes sense for a number of reasons. Borrowing rates typically exceed savings rates. Interest expense is usually nondeductible, while savings are taxable. Interest charges are a certainty, but investment returns are volatile.

Sure, these terms seems dry and boring. But let's face facts, it's not your father's economy anymore. In an era when consumer spending is high and there's plenty of new goods and services to buy that weren't available even 20 years ago, knowing how to budget properly is a big key to your financial success. According to a recent American Express consumer survey on everyday spending, today's list of typical, day-to-day expenses is still dominated by traditional items such as groceries, fast-food lunches, tolls, and gasoline. But they've been joined by certain 21st-century wallet-sappers such as cellular phone service, paging fees, and Internet service costs.

Consequently, as everyday expenses increase, managing a household budget becomes more complicated. The best solution? Get those costs into your budget as soon as possible, because people tend to spend whatever money is left over after paying the fixed expenditures and stop only when either the ATM won't give them more cash or the bank calls.

One way to keep money from flying out of your pocket is to write down what you're spending as you spend it. You may not realize it, but that glass of Merlot after work, the dry cleaning you picked up on the way home, and that four-cheese pizza you had delivered to your door for dinner all add up. A record of your daily, weekly, or monthly expenditures makes for some interesting reading in most American households, testing the patience of millions of spouses in the process.

As I've mentioned, some consumers like to use a credit card to buy everything (the credit card companies *LOVE* to push that strategy). That way, at the end of the month, they have a ready-made laundry list of expenditures sent to them by their credit card firm. Bad idea. Sure, you get a nice, clean list of what you spent each month. But getting into the habit of using a credit card is never a good ploy. It's easy to treat that Visa card like cash, but it ain't. Sooner or later you've got to pay for it, with high interest payments to boot if you're not on time every month. Besides, in the age of the laptop, it's easy to sit down at the end of the day and compile your own list. You'll have your record and you won't get sticker shock opening your credit card bill every month.

Budget Explained

Before I get into specific areas of your budget, let's take a brief look at how a normal household budget works. Primarily, all budgets are divided into income and expenses, but most good ones now include a third component, savings. Some items in the "income" section are after-tax salary, pensions, investments, and tax refunds.

Items in "expenditure" can include rent, mortgage payments, food, gas, utility bills, child care, entertainment, gifts, and holiday spending. The "savings" section logs how much you put away each month, after satisfying spending requirements. As much as 10 percent of total expenses should be put into this category to allow for unforeseeable events such as dental emergencies.

One way to attack your budget is to use what some debt counselors refer to as "the snowball method." Using this strategy, simply list your debts in ascending order with the smallest remaining balance first, the largest last. Do this regardless of interest rate or payment. You then pay these off in this new order. This works because you get to see some success quickly and are not trying to pay off the largest balance just because it has a high rate of interest.

Once you pay off the lowest balance, take that payment and combine it with the next payment on the list, so that each month you're making a larger payment on that debt. Repeat the process, again and again, so that your payments are getting larger, your debts are being paid off faster, and the process starts to snowball until all your debts are paid.

If you're one of those people who can't sleep at night worrying about bigger bills, go ahead and address those bills first. Just rank your debts in order of highest interest rate to lowest. Then whittle away at them in that order. Make sure you are not comparing apples and oranges. The effective interest rate is often different from the nominal rate quoted by the lender. For example, mortgage rates are compounded semiannually, while rates on credit card debt are usually compounded monthly.

Your Budget List

Here are some more tips on building a better budget:

1. Don't make your budget too restrictive. Otherwise, you might lose interest.
2. Use precise figures, not just estimates, so you know at any point exactly how much you need or have.
3. Consider using an Excel spreadsheet with two primary components—income and expenditure.
4. Budget sections should be easily understood. For example, include contractors and housepainters under Home Expenses. Better yet, paint the house yourself.
5. Don't underestimate what you spend. Figure in lunches that you eat in restaurants, movies (including Pay Per View at home) and other "extra" expenses.

6. Create and manage your budget on a monthly basis. Or build a budget that's based on how often you get paid.

7. Review your budget on a quarterly basis for accuracy—and to see how you're doing.

8. When the economy enters a low-interest-rate period, take advantage of low interest rates to refinance a home mortgage and make lower monthly payments. Numerous Web sites offer instant calculators that will estimate your new payments, including http://www.Quicken.com and http://www.realtor.com.

9. Add up the fees on your bank statements and shop for a better deal or ask your existing bank about lower-cost accounts. While you're at it, find out if your employer will automatically deposit your paycheck to your bank account, to minimize the risk of bounced checks and other mishaps. Consider starting an automatic savings plan that will route some money directly to a separate account before you're tempted to spend it.

10. Order a copy of your credit report for $8 from reporting agencies Equifax 800-685-1111, TransUnion 800-916-8800, or Experian 888-397-3742.

11. Eliminate clutter and raise extra cash by holding a garage sale or get a tax deduction by donating unwanted items to charities. In that case, be sure to keep an itemized receipt of donated goods in case the IRS has questions.

12. Make a detailed household inventory to protect yourself in case of theft or disaster. Engrave your name and an identifying code on high-value items, and record serial numbers. Most insurance companies offer guidelines or even workbooks—call yours or check out the Nationwide Mutual Insurance Company Web site at http://www.nationwide.com.

Above all, keep it fun. Open a bottle of wine, make a date with your loved one, flip a Dixie Chicks CD into your stereo. Saving money will put a smile on your face and make you feel good about yourself. It's time well spent.

Adding It Up

When you have filled in the sections of a budget table relevant to you, simply make totals of expenditure (including savings and investments) and income, and subtract expenditure from income. If your total is above zero, you are cash-flow positive. If the total is below zero, you are cash-flow negative. If the total is zero, you are cash-flow neutral.

If you end up with a positive cash flow, you can then consider investing the surplus, preferably in stocks or mutual funds. Or you can spend it. If you have a negative cash flow, you should examine what nonessential items you can eliminate.

The most common problem people have with budgets is sticking to them. Individuals who aren't very organized by nature need to have a more flexible budget, with broader categories such as "rent, entertainment, groceries, and bills" under expenses, rather than more detailed entries.

The last word on your budget. When you first start your budget, you should review it every pay period to see if you're on track. After that, review it when you do it—every month.

COOL ONLINE BUDGETING TOOLS

Online software is obviously a big help in managing your budget as well as your investment portfolio, but you should look for certain qualities. For example, regular viewers of those business and money TV shows on cable hear a lot about budget software packages like Quicken or Microsoft Money. The reason? Both include household accounting functions in addition to their investment portfolio tools.

If you don't want to spend the $50 or so that is required to buy such a software package, there's always the World Wide Web. While the list of personal financial planning Web sites available runs long and deep, a few sites in general offer some stable budgeting and family finance advice.

Some sites I recommend include:

Quicken Financial Network (http://www.qfn.com). Easy to learn and easy to use. Does loan payment calculations in addition to budgeting. Plus, it provides good tips and research sections.

FinanCenter (http://www.financenter.com/budget.htm). Fairly highbrow stuff. That said, the site has some cool calculators for figuring out your financial situation, particularly in the areas of budgeting and spending. The site offers some good overall financial tutorials, as well.

MetLife Online (http://www.metlife.com). The folks that brought you the Snoopy ads have a great site for everyday financial living. Just made a major purchase? The site provides a financial calculator to help evaluate the financial impact on your life. The same story goes for major health expenditures—such as surgery for a loved one in your family—or the impact of taking on a new job at a new salary.

Kiplinger.com (http://www.Kiplinger.com). From the same folks who bring you *Kiplinger's Personal Finance* magazine, the company Web site offers some good overall personal financial information in addition to its impressive roster of financial calculators.

The Dollar Stretcher (http://www.stretcher.com). This is a good site for the whole family. It has a great section on money and budgeting.

MONTHLY BUDGET CHECKLIST

Here's a ready-made list to keep track of your monthly expenditures:

Monthly Income

Net monthly salary/wages	$
Net monthly income from interest and dividends	$
Other monthly income, e.g., family allowances and benefits	$
Total monthly income	$ 0.00

Monthly Expenditure

Living expenses	$
Rent/mortgage payments	$
Food and beverages	$
Utilities, e.g., electricity, water	$
Clothing/footwear	$
Daily expenses, e.g., lunches	$
Household expenses	$
Insurance, e.g., house and contents, life	$
Health	$
Personal care, e.g., druggist, hairdresser	$
Medical, e.g., doctor, dentist, optician	$
Health insurance	$
Transportation	$
Gas	$
Repairs and maintenance	$
Registration, license, service clubs	$
Public transportation, taxis, parking	$
Vehicle insurance	$
Other	$
Children's expenses	$
Recreation, e.g., sports and activities	$
Entertainment, e.g., dining out, movies, books	$
Education, e.g., courses, associations	$
Gifts, e.g., presents, donations	$
Credit/loan repayments	$
Credit cards/charge account repayments	$
Rentals, paperwork, deeds, and legal documents	$
Personal loan repayments	$
Savings and investments	$
Unexpected events, replacements, additions	$
Savings, special goals, holidays, etc.	$
Investments in shares, properties, etc.	$
Total monthly expenditure	$ 0.00
Totals	
Total monthly income	$ 0.00
Total monthly expenditure	$ 0.00
Cash-flow position +/-	$ 0.00
+/-	

BEFORE YOU PAY OFF YOUR STUDENT LOAN, BUILD A PERSONAL FINANCE SYSTEM

Planning to pay off your student loan debt isn't a 100-yard dash, it's a marathon. Consequently, we have to take a champion marathoner's mind-set as we build the financial foundations that will support us throughout our lives. That means getting in good fiscal shape so we can tackle our student loan debt head on.

Part of that preparation is calculating your loan debt, building a budget, and creating a personal balance sheet—things I talked about already. The second half of the preparation phrase is the grist I'll use for the rest of this chapter, things such as creating a system and keeping track of your records and paperwork. I know, I know. There's no glamour or cachet in keeping tabs on your loan debt or calculating how much cash you'll need to pay off this debt. But as any Olympic marathoner will tell you, the race isn't won on marathon day. It's won in the preceding weeks when the real heavy lifting takes place, the road training, the diet, and the mental preparation.

CREATE A FILE SYSTEM

Start your organization campaign by creating a file system that makes it easy to get a loan statement or a canceled check at a moment's notice. Begin by saving all your student loan documents and all your correspondence from your lending institution. Also make sure you jot down names and numbers from any phone calls between you and your lender.

Set up an easy-to-use recordkeeping system to store your student loan documents and correspondence. Many books and software products on personal finance are available to help you get started. Whether you use file folders, portfolios, binders, or envelopes, it is a good idea to set up one folder for each type of loan or account and keep the items sorted accordingly.

Key Items to File

Certain items that should be included in your files are as follows:

- Documents such as your applications, promissory notes, disbursement and disclosure statements, and loan transfer notices
- Copies of all correspondence between you and your lender(s), loan holder(s), and/or servicer(s), and your school's financial aid office
- Up-to-date addresses and telephone numbers of your lender(s), loan holder(s), and/or servicer(s)
- The name of anyone you spoke to regarding your student loans, the date and time of the conversation, and a summary of what you discussed for future reference or clarification

Filing Tips

Where should you store everything? These days, just about everyone has a separate room in his or her house or apartment, or at least in the corner of the bedroom or the dining room, with a desk, maybe a personal computer, and some space to pay bills and conduct personal business. If you open your mail in the kitchen, keep a file drawer handy. If you have a home office, get an in box for bills and other personal mail. The key is not the sophistication of the space, but just having a dedicated place to handle your bills, your paperwork, and your money. Experts say a well setup work area or home office can help just about everyone reduce stress, improve productivity, and add more personal time every day.

More and more people are turning to multitask computer programs such as Quicken or Microsoft Money that automatically remind them of the bills to be paid, handle the math calculations, and make money management almost a pleasure. Plus, if you have a computer and a DSL line, or a dial-up modem, you can link your financial software to online services that let you keep track of your spending online. American Express cardholders, for example, can go to the Web site at http://www.americanexpress.com/cards to review recent charges, check balances, view their Membership Rewards points, download transactions into Quicken or Microsoft Money, and even pay their bills. A PC-based personal finance software package also eliminates what the American Bankers Association confirms as the single largest reason people overdraw their checking accounts: math errors. That's because money management software makes calculating balances a no-brainer even for those who aren't math experts.

Unfortunately, the personal computing era has done little to back up its claim as the gateway to the paperless era. Even with significant gains in the area of online bill payment and electronic trading and banking, paper documents in the form of student loan statements, bills, invoices, and the like are still very much with us, and will be until the day consumers finally demonstrate a wholesale trust and commitment to electronic-based personal finance. With the proliferation of computer bugs and viruses, particularly through the Internet and e-mail programs, that day isn't coming anytime soon.

In the meantime, organizing your paper documents is a must. You can start by keeping all your essentials in one spot. Keep most-used items—stamps, envelopes, stationery, file folders, and note pads—within arm's reach on your desk. If possible, place bookshelves and filing cabinets nearby. Create an in box for mail and a "to file" box. Post a running supply list to refer to when replenishing your stock.

Then go through all your financial records. Throw out all the records that you no longer need, such as old credit card statements, pay stubs, and ATM receipts that are more than a year old. Throw away the payment books from loans that are now paid off, including your car. Toss expired guarantees and warranties, and instruction manuals from items you've discarded or sold. You can also throw away most mutual fund statements you receive: keep only the consolidated annual report, which has a record of all the transactions from the year.

Be practical. Some papers are stored just for sentimental reasons. Ask yourself what's the worst thing that could happen if you threw the item away. If it is absolutely necessary, could you get another copy? If you really want something for just sentimental reasons, transfer it to your scrapbook or cedar chest.

One last thing. Shred the papers you plan to throw away. Your old personal papers are gold mines of information for thieves who may want your Social Security number or account numbers.

Okay, now you're organized and ready to tackle your student loan debt; you've got a plan in place to do just that. It's time to put that plan into action.

Student Loan Case Study

TROUBLE WAS IN THE CARDS

Michelle Bowren knew she had it coming. The 24-year-old public relations executive knew that when she was attending college, she was using her Visa card way too much. How much is too much? She left school with a credit card balance of $2,700.

"To me that was a fortune. I didn't have the nerve to tell my parents and I couldn't ask my boyfriend to help. I dug the hole for myself and I had to dig my way out."

Bowren used some gift money she received from her family for graduating and her year-end bonus at her public relations firm to finally pay off the bill, after one year of stress and worry.

"On one hand, I'm glad I paid off the bill," she says. "On the other, I could kick myself because I could have used the bonus money to help pay off my student loan or buy a nice used car. Instead, I had to use it to pay off my credit card—things I did and forgot about using the darned thing."

CHAPTER REVIEW

- On average, college students owe 33 percent more on their student loans now than students did in 1990.
- The first step in paying your student loan debt is facing up to it.
- Credit card debt is a student loan payer's worst enemy.
- Build a budget and develop a recordkeeping system before you begin to pay off your loan debt.

2

KNOW YOUR RIGHTS, KNOW THE PLAYERS, KNOW YOUR LOAN

There's really no secret on getting a grip on your student loan debt. It's all about getting the right information and acting on it. It's a good time to be looking for information, too. With the advent of the Internet, Google, and real-time technology, getting your hands on the information you need to bone up on your student loan is as easy as flipping open your laptop and firing up the World Wide Web.

It wasn't always so. In 1805, news of the British Fleet's victory at Trafalgar didn't reach New York City for six weeks. Nowadays, you might see 5,000 accounts of the battle and 50 Web logs dedicated to Admiral Nelson within six weeks.

So, thanks to the Information Age, where information is as much a commodity as vacuum cleaners or Viagra, we now have the most powerful weapon for learning right at our fingertips, just seconds away from being absorbed by our minds.

DIGGING IN

Okay, fine. But how does information apply to your student loan debt? Simple—it means everything. Things are tough enough when you leave school and embark on your professional life. There are jobs to land, apartments to rent, cars to buy, and other responsibilities that lay before you after graduation. The last thing you need is to deal with the biggest loan you've ever taken in your life, right?

But do it you must, and that's where the information issue comes into play. When you get out of school, you're probably not sure what city you'll be calling home in six months, let alone what your student loan responsibilities are. Even so, you need to bone up on who your lender is, what kind of loan you have, what terms like *deferment* and *guarantor* mean. You may find yourself buried under an avalanche of paperwork that would give a Tibetan Sherpa pause. And you may find yourself in complex discussions with loan specialists that make nuclear fission look easily understood.

But getting the right information makes that paperwork easier to handle and those conversations with your lender easier to comprehend. Consequently, arming yourself with the knowledge needed to manage your student loan debt lays the groundwork for the actual elimination of that debt. By knowledge, I mean knowing what your responsibilities are, who your lender is, what type of loan you have, and how to structure your debt elimination plan. Let's have a look.

YOUR RESPONSIBILITIES

When you accept the terms of a student loan it's easy to get caught up in the moment. After all, you'll be using the money to advance your learning, obtain a degree from an upstanding institution of higher knowledge, and contribute to society and make the world a better place after you graduate and embark upon your career.

All of these things are worthwhile and good. But it's helpful to remember that, all high-mindedness aside, your lending institution has a different view of your loan. To them it's a business arrangement, a deal, a contract, and a way for them to make some money.

Some sage once said that a "cigar was just a cigar," meaning that often things are just what they appear to be. In your case, a loan is just a loan—something to take responsibility for and something to work hard to pay back after all the cap-and-gown hoopla at good old Whattsamatta U.

When the din dies down and you've got your diploma, it's time to refocus on those responsibilities. In a nutshell, you took the loan with the understanding that you would pay it back according to the terms of the agreement, whether you finish school or not or whether you land a job after you graduate or not. That's no obligation to take lightly. If you don't pay your loan, or *default* in the parlance of the loan industry, you're setting the stage for financial disaster for the remainder of your life (or until you finally pay off the debt).

While I'll delve more deeply in the issue of default in Chapter 5, suffice to say that default is a DefCon Five, high-alert, is-there-a-doctor-in-the-house, full-blown panic situation for an individual who bails out on his or her loan obligations.

Let's try this another way. In mathematical terms, default is a formula for lifelong financial trauma. As in: blow off loans = default + bad credit = no homeownership + no new car × no credit card = lousy life.

Get the picture?

So take those loan obligations seriously. Even if you don't, the lending institution will, and they'll want their money back. In fact, they'll want it back so bad that they'll hound you like a dog, stick to you like a barnacle to the hull of a boat, and be like bubble gum on your shoe until they get their money back—or ruin your financial life if they don't. Believe me, lending institutions aren't charitable institutions. They have absolutely no problem making your life miserable if you're slow or a no-show in paying off your loan.

Also remember that when you take out a student loan, you have certain responsibilities. Primary among those responsibilities is your promise to pay back the money you borrowed. As stated by the U.S. Department of Education in the *Student Guide*—1996–1997:

> When you sign a *promissory note,* you're agreeing to repay the loan according to the terms of the note. The note is a binding legal document and states that, except in cases of loan discharge, you must repay the loan—even if you don't complete your education (unless you were unable to complete your program of study because the school closed); you aren't able to get a job after you complete the program; or are dissatisfied with, or don't receive, the education you paid for.

Some other responsibilities you have as a student loan borrower—and the excuses you cannot use—are as follows:

I never got the bill. Sorry, but not receiving a bill or loan statement in the mail is not grounds for not paying your student loan bill. Lending rules state that loan recipients must make payments on their student loans even if they do not receive bills or repayment notices.

I need more time. Sometimes you hit a rough patch and you can't pay your student loan bills perhaps for months at a time. In those instances, it's a good idea to ask for a deferment or a forbearance—basically a "loan holiday" when you don't have to pay your student loans until you get your financial act together. If, that is, your lending institution goes along with your request. But, according to the U.S. Department of Education, if you request such a delay you still have to make payments until you are notified that the request has been granted. If you stop paying on your loan anyway, you could be in default. A tip: Keep copies of all deferment request correspondence because they could come in handy if your loan is in question later on.

I thought you had a crystal ball. When you graduate from school, transfer to a new school, or drop out or attend as a part-time student, it's your responsibility to let your lending institution know about it.

I didn't think it was that time of the month. Your loan payments are expected each month.

YOUR RIGHTS AS A BORROWER

When you accept the conditions of a student loan and sign on the dotted line, then, by law, you become the holder of certain in-alienable rights, too. For instance, it's up to the lender to provide you with the following loan data:

- The complete amount of the loan
- Your loan's interest rate
- When you must start repaying the loan
- The effect borrowing will have on your eligibility for other types of financial aid
- A tally of any charges you must repay (loan fees) and infor-mation on how those charges are collected
- The annual and total amounts you can borrow
- The maximum repayment periods and the minimum repay-ment amount
- The straight skinny on default and its consequences
- Information on debt consolidation and/or refinancing

Note, too, that because you are a student loan recipient, the lending institution must give you a grace period before you have to start paying off your debt. Your original loan contract should stipulate the specifics of your grace period. Or contact your lending institution for the information.

You also have the right to a loan repayment schedule provided by your lender, stipulating when your first payment is due, how often you have to pay, and the amount you'll be paying with each installment.

Your lender must also:

- Give you a prespecified time limit to repay your loan
- Allow you to prepay your loan at any time without penalty
- Cancel if you become permanently disabled or kick the bucket
- Provide you with a "graduated" loan payment option where you pay less at the start (because money will likely be tighter when you are 25 than at 35) and pay more later as your income rises
- Provide you with an extended repayment schedule of up to 25 years, but only if you are a Federal Family Education Loan Program (FFELP) borrower whose debt exceeds $30,000. You also must have no outstanding FFELP principal or interest as of October 7, 1998, or on the date an FFELP loan is obtained after October 7, 1998.

L o a n   **S** *n a p s h o t*

BARE NAKED MINIMUM

Most student loans offer a minimum monthly payment of $50 or so. So if you're short of funds one month, and you can't afford to pay the full freight, send the minimum amount. Your lender will appreciate the effort and it's much better than paying nothing at all.

THE PLAYERS

Who takes center stage on student loans? Well, you are on one side and a public or private lending institution is on the other. Who are these other players and what roles do they play in the loan process? Let's take a look.

Federal government. Yes, Uncle Sam, under the official guise of the U.S. Department of Education, runs the federal student loan programs. The federal government can be either a lender or a guarantor, which is an institution that guarantees your loan.

Borrower. You, basically, unless your mom, dad, grandmother, or grandfather have signed off on your student loan. The borrower is the person who gets the student loan and is obligated to pay it off.

Lender. The institution that cuts you the check for your student loan. A lender can be the government, a bank, a credit union, or another financial institution. Here's a list of potential lenders:

- Bank
- Savings and loan association
- School
- Credit union
- Pension fund
- Insurance company
- Consumer finance company
- Federal government

Your school. Don't forget old alma mater. Your school can identify financial aid options, figure out how much you need, help you get the loan, and administer it. They're also on the back end when you have to pay the loan when you leave.

The guarantor. Usually a federal agency that guarantees to your lending institution that you'll actually pay back the money you borrowed. If you don't pay off the loan, the guarantor has to.

The credit bureau. The private agency that keeps tabs on your loan payments and makes your "credit score" available to others interested in your ability to pay back money that you owe. That could be a mortgage company, or a retail store, or an automobile dealer—in short, anyone who is going to make a financial commitment with you.

The collection agency. The agency that will come after you, sent by the guarantor, if you default on your loans and make no arrangements to pay them back. Usually, the collection agency earns about 30 percent of your total outstanding loan if they can get you to pay it back.

The credit counselor. In some cases, you might need professional advice on getting out of student loan debt. A reputable credit counselor can show you how to rearrange or consolidate your loans so you're not in default. Not all credit counselors are reputable, though (more on that in Chapter 7).

TYPES OF STUDENT LOANS

Student loans are like ice cream—there are myriad flavors, but two or three are by far the big sellers. Basically, student loans are broken down into two primary categories: needs-based loans (usually government loans) and non–needs-based loans (usually from banks and other private lenders). Of the two groups, needs-based, or government loans, are by far the most common student loans.

The Difference between Government and Nongovernment Loans

It doesn't square with the way that Uncle Sam usually does business, but the primary difference between government loans and non-government loans is that with the former, you don't have to start paying off interest on your loan right away. With private loans, you usually do.

Private loans also typically require you to assign a guarantor (a cosigner) to your loan. Again, the U.S. government offers the easier option (in most cases) in not requiring a cosigner for your loan. That's a big advantage for a young college student who's not sitting on a pile of dough and whose last name isn't Vanderbilt, Carnegie, or Gates.

The good news with private loans is that you can usually negotiate a lower interest rate from the bank whose loan you're considering. That's especially true if you're able to convince your parents or grandparents to act as guarantors on your loan.

Here is a look at the most common loans from both groups.

Guaranteed Student Loans (GSLs), or Stafford Loans

Guaranteed Student Loans (GSLs), more commonly known as Stafford loans, are guaranteed by the federal government, meaning you will always receive your fund income no matter what is happening in the economic world. Stafford loans are popular primarily because they have a lower interest rate than most other varieties of loans.

By and large, there are two classes of Stafford loans. *Subsidized* Stafford loans are available to students who have shown need as determined by their financial aid applications. The federal government subsidizes the loan by not charging any interest until six months after the student graduates, leaves school, or falls below half-time attendance status.

The second type of Stafford loan is known as *unsubsidized* and is not based on need. Virtually all students are eligible for these loans. From the moment a student takes out an unsubsidized Stafford loan, however, he or she will be charged interest. Students are given the option of paying the interest while in school or deferring interest payments (which will continue to accrue) until repayment of principal begins.

In both cases the federal government guarantees the loan, which ensures a very low interest rate. (Today, the in-school interest rate is 7.59 percent!) The dependent student may be eligible to borrow up to $2,625 for the freshman year, up to $3,500 for the sophomore year, and up to $5,500 per year for the remaining undergraduate years. Graduate students can borrow up to $18,500 per year; however, only a maximum of $8,000 per year will be available with a subsidized Stafford.

Most lending institutions use a loan interest rate that is tied to the U.S. government's Treasury bill rate, specifically the 91-day T-bill. That rate changes annually each July. Careful, though. The Stafford loan's interest rate varies depending on where you are in your education. Still in school? Okay, the rate is the T-bill plus 1.70 percent. Out of school? The rate is the T-bill plus 2.30 percent. On Wall Street, bond traders call those individual rate percentiles *basis points.* So you're paying 60 more basis points (2.30 percent to 1.70 percent) in paying off your loan after you graduate than before you graduate. In layman's terms that means you usually have to pay 6 percent or 7 percent interest on your Stafford loan. By law, the rate for Stafford loans can never exceed 8.25 percent.

Stafford loans are easy to get but you are expected to pay them off within ten years. You can obtain a loan through Uncle Sam's Direct Lending program or you can go through a participating bank—and most banks do participate.

L o a n   S n a p s h o t

FEDERAL STAFFORD LOANS—NEEDY AND NOT

There are two types of federal Stafford loans: subsidized and unsubsidized. Here is how they break down:

Subsidized. Subsidized loans are needs-based. The federal government pays the interest on these loans while the student is in school and during the grace period before repayment begins.

Unsubsidized. These loans are available for students who don't qualify for subsidized loans. You, the borrower, are responsible for the interest on this loan as soon as it is taken out. Most of the terms and conditions of subsidized and nonsubsidized Stafford loans are the same.

L o a n   S n a p s h o t

WATCH THE FEES, PLEASE

You can save some serious bucks on your student loan by negotiating fees with your lending institution—even if you haven't paid your loan yet. Normally, lenders stick you with an *origination fee* of up to 3 percent of the loan's balance and an additional 1 percent *administrative fee* that usually goes to the loan guarantor. It can't hurt to ask your lender to cut or rebate this fee—many of them are now doing so. But you really have to ask.

Direct Student Loans (Perkins Loans)

Direct Student Loans, so called because they are administered by the school you attend, offer even better interest rate deals than do Stafford loans (which aren't too shabby in the first place).

Now more commonly known as Perkins loans, direct loans are made straight to you, the student, and often carry an agreeable interest rate of about 5 percent. You don't have to begin repaying your Perkins loan until you graduate or leave school and even then you have a grace period of six to nine months. Recordkeeping is easy, as long as you're in school, because your academic institution usually administers your loan right through its bursar's or finance office. Even after you graduate you can still call your school for questions on the loan.

Eligibility requirements for Perkins loans are fairly simple. You have to be a U.S. citizen and either a full- or part-time student. There are limits as to how much you can borrow with a Perkins loan: $4,000 is the cap for one year and $20,000 is the cap for your duration in college (for undergraduates).

L o a n   S n a p s h o t

WHERE DO YOU RATE?

Interest rates on student loans aren't pie-in-the-sky numbers—they're actually based on carefully calculated financial indexes. For the record, your student loan is likely pegged on either the U.S. prime interest rate or the U.S. Treasury bill rate. Don't know the rates? Check your local newspaper or favorite business-oriented Web site. The U.S. Bureau of the Public Debt is a good site. Find it at: http://www.publicdebt.treas.gov.

Federal Parent Loans for Undergraduate Students (PLUS)

Parents who want more control over their child's student loan have an option known as the federal Parent Loan for Undergraduate Students—or PLUS. The beauty of the PLUS is twofold: It enables parents to fund the complete cost of their child's education, including books, meals, and such. And it allows them to do so at a fair interest rate—about 4 percent in recent years. Plus, no pun intended, the rate of the parent loans cannot—again by law—exceed 9 percent.

PLUS offers some additional advantages. They

- are not based on income or assets,
- require no collateral,
- have interest that may be tax-deductible,
- offer a ten-year window to repay the loan,
- offer no prepayment penalty, and
- offer loan amounts up to the total bill for the student's education.

Additional Types of Loans

While Stafford, Perkins, and PLUS loans are the most commonly used classes of student loans, they don't have the stage to themselves. Here are some other types of student loans that have found favor among borrowers.

Home equity loans. Equity loans offer the benefit of low interest rates and an interest deduction on your taxes. Plus, you're not tied down to any restrictions as with most other student loans. You can use the money to rent an apartment near campus, purchase a new computer, or even buy a used car to take you to class and back. Downside: no cap on interest rates, so payback can be a bear if interest rates are on the rise.

Private loans. Private education loans from banks, credit agencies, and other financial institutions are another option. Sallie Mae, for example, offers a private education loan through its Signature Education Loan Program—a team effort in which federal and private loans are available to students from a single lender. Big benefit: Borrowers get customer service from a single agency for the life of the loan (Sallie Mae, in this case). That means you write only one check to Sallie Mae no matter how many different student loans you have with the agency.

MBA, LAW, and MED loans. These are usually federal Stafford loans—with some private loan qualities depending on which lend-

FIGURE 2.1 *Student Loans by the Numbers*

Loan Type	Interest Rate	Loan Maximum	Grace Period
Perkins	Fixed at 5%	$3,000	9 months after school
Stafford	Variable— 8.25% cap	$5,500	6 months after school
Parent PLUS	Variable—9% cap	Open (based on need)	60 days after getting loan

ing institution a student uses—that cater to graduate students targeting a specific educational discipline. Really no big difference from traditional undergraduate loans because all cover the entire period spent in graduate school with similar interest rates and payment schedules as undergraduate loans.

Chances are that as a student loan borrower you received either a Stafford or Perkins loan, or possibly received some parental help in the form of a PLUS loan (for the number information on each type of these loans, see Figure 2.1).

Even so, knowing exactly what type of loan you have and what rights and responsibilities come attached to that loan is a key step in eliminating your student loan debt. Image may be everything in some circles, but when it comes to student loan debt, information is everything.

LOAN LINGO

Stumped by the terminology used by lenders? Don't be. Here is a list of the most common student loan terms and what they mean:

Borrower. In this case, you. The individual who is responsible for repaying a loan.

Capitalization. The interest that builds up over time and is added to your principal (otherwise known as "capitalized" interest). Be careful about capitalization, it can hike the total cost of your loan.

Consolidation. To merge some or all of your student loans into one *über* loan, with one interest rate and one payment per month. More on consolidation in Chapter 6.

Default. What happens if you fail to repay your loan. Usually a precursor to a bad credit rating and, consequently, financial troubles in obtaining further loans to buy a home or a car or go back to school again.

Deferment. A delay of payments on your student loan. To gain a deferment, a lender may make you prove "eligibility" criteria like being sick or unemployed.

Discharge. A release from your obligation to repay your loan permanently.

Fees. Additional expenses tacked to your total loan amount due, or subtracted from the amount of money you receive with your loan funds.

Forbearance. A time period when you can skate on your loan payments because of extenuating conditions and you do not qualify for a deferment.

Grace period. A six- or nine-month period after you leave school and have to start making regular payments on your student loans.

Interest. The fee you pay for the privilege of borrowing money from your lending institution (it's their profit margin). Interest is based on a percentage of your total loan.

Principal. The total amount you owe on your student loan.

S t u d e n t L o a n C a s e S t u d y

IF NOTHING ELSE, PAY THE MINIMUM

Kevin Kane was aware that those little envelopes were coming in the mail—the ones with the lending institution's name on them in big block letters and the little slip of paper inside demanding payment on his student loan.

"I couldn't get a job right out of college so I wound up bartending at night," says the 23-year-old computer software grad. "I knew they were looking for their money but I was just scraping by."

One afternoon, Kane's girlfriend, Patty, stopped by and noticed the unopened bill. "She gave me that look like I had done something wrong," Kane says. "I figured I'd better own up and admit I hadn't been paying off my student loans."

The good news was that Patty had been in the same situation a year ago, and mentioned that by paying the minimum, she bought enough time until she got her financial act together and could pay more.

"She told me she had paid the minimum $50 for four months in a row last year," he added. "I figured that I could manage that."

Soon after, Kane began shipping out $50 per month to pay his student loan debt. Six months later, he found a good-paying job and bumped up his payments accordingly.

"I hate it when my girlfriend's right, but she saved my bacon that time," he says. "By paying the minimum I had enough time to get a good job and get going."

CHAPTER REVIEW

- Know your rights as a borrower.
- Know your obligations as a borrower.
- Know who the players are in your loan picture.
- Know what types or types of student loans you have—and what their terms are.

3

TIME TO PAY THE PIPER

In and of itself, money is one hell of an education. In fact, if you don't know anything about money, you can learn all about it by going down to the bank and borrowing some. And then having to pay it back again. With interest. Which, with your student loan, is pretty much what you did.

That's okay, though. As I've said, taking out a student loan is a great way to invest in your own future. Chances are, the education you receive will lead to a career that will more than pay off any student loan debt.

Besides, long term, money isn't as important as you think it is. True, as boxer Joe Louis once said, "Money doesn't mean much to me, but it does calm my nerves." But the real measure of a life well lived isn't money, it's family, friends, and fulfillment.

Unfortunately, for the short term, you're going to be thinking lots and lots about money as you pay off your student loan debt. So while the three *Fs* I just mentioned are important, they really come into play when you get closer to your Golden Years and reflect upon life—not when you're young and preparing for it. For now, thinking about money—specifically thinking how it's going to get you out of student loan debt—is no luxury. It's a necessity.

FRAMING YOUR LOAN PICTURE

Okay, let's review. We've set up a recordkeeping system and a budget, identified the type of loan you're likely dealing with, and detailed the rights and responsibilities you have as a loan borrower. Now it's time to use all these tools to begin paying off your student loan. Let's get going.

THE LIFE STAGES OF YOUR LOAN

Life Stages is a very popular term these days, particularly on Wall Street, the industry that I hail from. There, the term is meant to encompass the various eras or stages of your life from a financial point of view—going to college, finding your first job, getting married, buying your first home, having kids—right on down the line to retirement. The idea is that you should identify the various stages of your life and develop a financial plan to deal with them. At least that's what Wall Street firms hope you will do. That way they can collect the hefty fees from all those big financial moves you're making.

From a student loan standpoint, a life stages view is just as useful, although not as sinister as the kind you see in the financial services sector. In a student loan life cycle, you start the ball rolling by researching your loan options, applying for one (or more), accepting a loan, going to school and graduating, and then the last part of the cycle—paying off your loan—begins. All told, the life stages thing can last up to 15 years or so, from the time you start looking for a loan to when you actually pay it off.

Well, paying off a loan is where we are in Chapter 3.

LOAN LIFE STAGES

Here is how your typical student loan life cycle plays out. By and large, it begins when you're as young as 17 (when you start researching loan options) and ends in your mid-30s (when you finish paying off those loans if you went to grad school).

The Early Phase—The Research Cycle

- You, along with your parents or guardian, begin researching financial aid options.
- You're accepted at school.
- You begin the process of discovering what you can pay for on your own (with savings) and with nonloan financial aid (scholarships, grants, tuition breaks).
- The gap left between what you have to pay for and what you can afford to pay for is the amount of estimated money you'll need in student loans.
- You begin the process of researching student loans.
- You identify the loan you want and complete and submit your application.
- Your lender approves your loan.

The Middle Phase

- A check is cut by the lending institution and delivered to your home or straight to your school's financial office.
- The school takes what it needs to cover your tuition, room and board, and other expenses, and returns the remaining amount to you.

- The lending institution sends its first disclosure statement to your home (likely your parents' home). This is particularly true for federal PLUS loans.
- The lender notifies the credit bureau that the loan has been transacted.
- You attend school, during which time you are not obligated to make any student loan payments.

The Last Phase

- You complete your education, hopefully with a cap-and-gown affair upon graduation. Or you leave school early.
- You enter your grace period when you have, on average, from six to nine months before your first loan payment is due.
- Your lending institution, during this grace period, sends you a repayment disclosure statement detailing your loan obligations and the timetable for repaying them.
- When the grace period ends, you receive your first bill, usually a monthly one.
- You begin paying your student loans.
- If all goes well, you pay each month—or even prepay—until your loan is paid off.
- Your lending institution confirms that your loan obligation has been fulfilled.
- Your lending institution sends confirmation to credit bureaus that the loan has been retired.

PREPARING TO PAY

It's at the last phase that we're starting. Now that you've left school and earned your degree, you must pay back your loan money. Hopefully, you want to start the loan repayment process with the blueprint we covered in Chapter 1.

This means gathering all your loan documentation that you so carefully stored so you know exactly how much you owe, how much you're going to have to pay each month, and what your final loan obligation is. You also must know where to mail your check. Normally, your lender will send you a monthly invoice detailing exactly where the money should go.

Thus, you should have the following loan documents on hand (see Chapter 1 for more details):

- Any loan applications, promissory notes, loan statements, and loan transfer notices This information should be kept readily accessible.
- All correspondence between you and your lender. Keep documents from your school's financial aid office, too.
- Exact addresses, phone numbers, and e-mail contacts of your lending institution. Again, the same information is helpful for contacting your school's financial aid office.
- Exact names of any contacts you may have already spoken to at your lending institution or at school. Having a good contact is a real boost—when you have a question or a problem, you can start by contacting that person directly and go from there. A friendly face always helps.

KNOW YOUR PROMISSORY NOTE

In the previous list I mention the term *promissory note*. I know it sounds dry and wonkish, but it's a term you should know. When you borrow money from a lender, that lender will want you to sign a contract stipulating just who is going to do what, when, and in what amount. In other words, a promissory note.

A promissory note says that you swear on a stack of Bibles to repay the loan under the terms agreed to within the loan. Because a promissory note is a legal document, you need to understand how it can impact you down the road. So read it, maybe have a lawyer read it, or someone knowledgeable about contract law in your school's financial aid department, and make sure you understand what it means before you agree to the contract.

What's a promissory note comprised of? Contract particulars include the amount you are borrowing, the interest rate and fees tied into the loan, the time frame of the repayment period, and under what circumstances fees and collection costs may be added to your student loan bill.

NOT PAYING? SORRY, NOT YOUR BEST OPTION

When you signed your promissory note and accepted your student loan, you pledged that you would pay back the money. By meeting that obligation, you gain the type of credit that will enable you to buy homes, lease cars, send your own children to school one day, and all that other good stuff that comes from having good financial credit.

But what if you don't repay your loan? Bad news. If you don't pay off your loan you get branded with the *D* word—as in default (or debtor, too, for that matter). The downside of default includes years of bad credit rating, garnishment of wages to pay your student loans (you didn't think the lender would give up that easily, did you?), seizure of tax refunds, and pile upon pile of added interest rate and administrative (late charge) fees.

Call it spiritual debtor's prison, where the lender locks up your financial life for years and throws away the key. No warden, either. So, it's always best to pay your debt. No matter what. But, if you absolutely can't pay, take heart. Later on in the book I'll go into great detail and discuss what to do if you can't pay your student loan.

Loan Snapshot

AMAZING GRACE

After you graduate or leave school, you have a grace period before you have to start paying your loan. Here are the grace periods for the most common types of student loans:

Federal (FFEL) or Direct Stafford loans = Six months
Federal Perkins loans = Nine months
Direct PLUS loans = 60 days after loan is disbursed

PAYING OFF YOUR LOAN

Where do your student loans fit into your financial lifestyle? That's the first question you have to ask when you start paying off your loan. The answer can be found in three facts, which we touched upon in Chapter 2:

1. The size of your loan
2. The length of your repayment time frame
3. Your loan's interest rate

Loan Repayment Options

A humorist once said that there are two things about a bill: always question it and never pay it until you've exhausted all the other options. Funny, yes, but not a strategy that will have fortune smiling on you when all is said and done.

No, the options I'm talking about here are your repayment options. These are the different methods of repaying your loan, depending on what type of loan you received, what your obligations are for repaying that loan, and the timetable for doing so (see Figure 3.1 for sample monthly payments).

FIGURE 3.1 *Sample Monthly Student Loan Payments**

Amount Borrowed	Number of Payments	Monthly Payment
$2,625	60	$53.54
3,500	60	71.39
5,250	72	92.69
5,250	120	64.39

*Based on 8.25% interest rate

Let's examine the most common loan repayment options.

Standard repayment. In a standard loan repayment scenario, you just pay the principal and interest that has accrued on your loan, usually on a monthly basis for the duration of the loan repayment term. A standard loan repayment option is by far the most common form of paying back student loans. You pay back your loan in equal monthly payments over, for example, a ten-year period, or 120 equal payments. The minimum monthly payment might be as low as $50, but the actual monthly cost depends on your loan balance and interest rate.

Let's say, hypothetically, that you borrowed $20,684, which includes the full amount of the debt, plus interest. With a standard repayment schedule, your monthly obligation to your student loan lender would be $174 per month for ten years.

The beauty of the standard repayment schedule is that it runs like clockwork. The bill arrives on the same day every month for the same amount. It's simple, but simple is good when your life grows complicated after college.

Graduated repayment. With graduated repayments, you start small and work your way up. As I mentioned before, lenders understand that, chances are, you won't be a lean, mean big paycheck-making machine when you first get out of school. Your big earning years will come later. To accommodate that reality, lenders offer graduated payment plans by which your loan can be paid off in smaller and then increasingly larger regular amounts as you earn more money. Of course, if you get a good-paying job right out of school, go ahead and pay as much as you can on your student loan. Remember that the idea is to pay it off as quickly as possible. That's not necessarily the case with graduated repayment plans.

If, for example, you snagged a student loan directly from the government, your starting payments may be half of what they would be under the standard plan (there is no minimum amount, but your payment can never be less than the monthly interest due). Then they'll increase every two years, for 10 to 30 years. Your monthly payments will never rise to more than 150 percent of what the monthly payments would be under the standard plan.

With other loans you might pay only the interest on your loans for a few years. After that you'll pay both principal and interest on the loan until it's retired.

Earnings-based payment. Again, lenders often get a bad rap that they have no heart and are after your money and little else. But with the earnings-based repayment plan, otherwise referred to as an "income-sensitive" plan, like the graduated repayment student loan plan, lenders acknowledge that everyone isn't paid like a Vanderbilt and that they will work with borrowers to come up with monthly bills that can accommodate the borrower's budget. As long as the lending institution is getting their money from you on a regular basis—even in smaller amounts as with the earnings-based payment plan—then they're relatively happy.

That said, there are some caveats involving income-sensitive loans. Repayment of your student loans under this option takes into consideration the amount of income you make, or your total gross monthly income. Your monthly payment is then based on the amount of your income. Under this option:

- You have to come absolutely clean about all you receive.
- The income information you give to your lender cannot be more than 90 days old.

- You don't make the call, your lending institution does. They determine whether you qualify for the income-sensitive repayment option.
- Your payment plan is liable for review annually by your lender.

Extended repayment. Not the ideal repayment option for the student borrower, the extended repayment plan factors in long periods of time when you can't pay your student loan and gives you more time to do so. About 25 years of time. So if you are disabled or lose your job and can't find another one, the lender will "string out" your loan timetable up to 25 years. Of course, as they do that, your lender will string out and increase the interest payments you'll be paying as well. Still, it's nice to have an extended option in your back pocket if things break down, which hopefully won't happen.

Postponing Repayment

If your loan payments are huge or if you've hit tough economic times head on, even the most generous payment plan might not make ends meet. In some instances, you can—for the moment at least—postpone paying your loans or reduce the amount of your payments. These periods of relief are known as deferments (when Uncle Sam pays your interest) and forbearances (when the money you owe keeps going up because interest payments aren't being paid). I'll talk more about deferments and forbearances in Chapter 5.

Additional Repayment Options

The repayment express doesn't stop there. There are plenty of other ways to pay your bill and shed that student loan albatross from your shoulders. Check these out and see if there's a place for one or two in your student loan repayment plan.

STAFFORD LOANS AND INCOME-SENSITIVE OPTIONS

Not every lender treats income loan repayment the same. Under federal direct Stafford or consolidation loans, you are usually eligible for an income-based repayment plan. PLUS loans, however, are not eligible. The amount you pay annually on income-based loans differs, but it will never exceed 20 percent of your discretionary income—that is, your annual gross income less an amount based on the poverty level for your household size.

Prepaying. There's an old saying in the financial world that "There's no rule that says you have to spend any raise you get at work." Similarly, there's no rule that says you can't pay your loan off before its full amount is due.

Both proverbs, as it were, are on the spot in the sense that financial benefits come to those who think creatively. Remember, the longer it takes to pay your student loan debt, the more interest you'll pay. You can't do much about the amount of money you borrowed—the principal—but you can do something about the bank account–sapping interest you pay on your loan. By paying it off early, you kill those onerous interest payments. In the process you're taking money that could have gone to the bank off the table and putting it back where it belongs—in your pocket.

Loan Snapshot

"ON TIME" PAYMENTS

Paying on time and regularly has hidden benefits, too. Some lenders reward regular on-time payments with interest rate reductions. That could save you thousands of dollars over the life of your loan.

Bank deductions. There is no shortage of lending institutions that enable you to make student loan payments automatically from your bank account. Besides being convenient, automatic bank transfers help you maintain a good credit rating by ensuring on-time payments. Some lenders may even offer a decrease in the interest rate on your student loans just by going for the automatic deduction.

L o a n   S n a p s h o t

SCHEDULE YOUR PAYMENTS

You can tailor, with minimal effort, the monthly date you receive your student loan bill. For instance, if you are paid monthly on the 30th, you can ask your lender to send your bill on the first of the month. That way you should have enough on hand to pay your loan bill.

In Figure 3.2 is a sample student loan repayment table, based on a student loan of $5,000, with an interest rate of 5 percent. Total interest is $1,281.30; total amount to repay is $6,281.30—assuming all payments are made as scheduled. Payments began September 1, 1998.

L o a n   S n a p s h o t

REPAYMENT TIPS

Like most things in life, think before you sign on the dotted line. For example, you can pay off your loan sooner if you add $10 or $20 per monthly payment. You'll hardly miss the money but you can shave months, if not a year or two, off your loan schedule by doing so.

FIGURE 3.2 *Student Loan Repayment Table*

Due Date	Principal Due	Interest Due	Total Due
1. 9/1/1998	$ 125.00	$ 62.50	$ 187.50
2. 12/1/1998	125.00	60.94	185.94
3. 3/1/1999	125.00	59.38	184.38
4. 6/1/1999	125.00	57.81	182.81
5. 9/1/1999	125.00	56.25	181.25
6. 12/1/1999	125.00	54.69	179.69
7. 3/1/2000	125.00	53.13	178.13
8. 6/1/2000	125.00	51.56	176.56
9. 9/1/2000	125.00	50.00	175.00
10. 12/1/2000	125.00	48.44	173.44
11. 3/1/2001	125.00	46.88	171.88
12. 6/1/2001	125.00	45.31	170.31
13. 9/1/2001	125.00	43.75	168.75
14. 12/1/2001	125.00	42.19	167.19
15. 3/1/2002	125.00	40.63	165.63
16. 6/1/2002	125.00	39.06	164.06
17. 9/1/2002	125.00	37.50	162.50
18. 12/1/2002	125.00	35.94	160.94
19. 3/1/2003	125.00	34.38	159.38
20. 6/1/2003	125.00	32.81	157.81
21. 9/1/2003	125.00	31.25	156.25
22. 12/1/2003	125.00	29.69	154.69
23. 3/1/2004	125.00	28.13	153.13
24. 6/1/2004	125.00	26.56	151.56
25. 9/1/2004	125.00	25.00	150.00
26. 12/1/2004	125.00	23.44	148.44
27. 3/1/2005	125.00	21.88	146.88
28. 6/1/2005	125.00	20.31	145.31
29. 9/1/2005	125.00	18.75	143.75
30. 12/1/2005	125.00	17.19	142.19
31. 3/1/2006	125.00	15.63	140.63
32. 6/1/2006	125.00	14.06	139.06
33. 9/1/2006	125.00	12.50	137.50
34. 12/1/2006	125.00	10.94	135.94
35. 3/1/2007	125.00	9.38	134.38
36. 6/1/2007	125.00	7.81	132.81
37. 9/1/2007	125.00	6.25	131.25
38. 12/1/2007	125.00	4.69	129.69
39. 3/1/2008	125.00	3.13	128.13
40. 6/1/2008	125.00	1.56	126.56
Totals	**$5,000.00**	**$1,281.30**	**$6,281.30**

Source: University of Wisconsin, Bursar's Office, http://www.bussvc.wisc.edu/bursar/sked5.html.

MORE TIPS ON STUDENT LOAN PAYMENTS

Let's talk about some more tips on repaying your student loans. All are designed to help you get to the Holy Grail of student loan debt—the day you make your last student loan payment. Put some of these ideas to work and see if that day doesn't come sooner than you think.

Don't wait for a bill to come from your lender every month. Go ahead and send a check regardless of whether you receive a bill or not. It's habit forming and therapeutic, in the sense that you're cutting your debt down to size. People who wait for the bill to come are taking, in my opinion, a passive approach to student loan debt. By taking charge and cutting a check no matter what, you're taking command over your own fiscal situation. And that's a habit that will pay off over the course of your lifetime.

Know all the repayment options available from your lender. Make sure that the repayment option fits your current financial situation. If you're flush with cash, go ahead and pay more than you owe. If not, work with your lender to accommodate a financial dry spell with a different loan repayment plan. Like anything else, when it comes to debt, knowledge is power.

Keep your lender in the loop. If you move, get married, or even change your phone number, let your lender know. Direct contact is the easiest and best way to solve any problems that arise. But you have to know who to reach. And the lender has to know how to reach you.

Take a break before starting graduate school. If you're planning on going straight to graduate school but don't have the money to pay the bills, try taking a year or two off and go into the corporate world to earn some money. After that, you'll have earned enough to defray any further student loan costs. Bonus: By taking time off between schools and spending some time working for a living, you'll gain a greater appreciation of what you want to do with your life—and what you might want to study when you return to grad school.

Request a deferment. If you do attend graduate school, request a deferment from your lender from any undergraduate student loans. As long as you are in grad school, you won't be receiving any bills for your student loan from your undergraduate days. But work closely with your lender to make sure you filed all the proper paperwork to gain that deferment. Note that it's much easier to defer government loans than it is private loans. Again, if you are in graduate school at least try to make interest payments on your undergraduate student loan. That will defray the total cost of the loan and help you develop good repayment habits.

Use gift money. Remember the scene in *The Graduate* when people came up to Dustin Hoffman and offered congratulations and encouragement for his graduating from college? If you looked closely, you'd have noticed them giving him an envelope or two in the process, containing hefty checks, no doubt. If you are similarly rewarded with a bonus from relatives and friends for graduation, or received a signing bonus to work for a firm right out college, use it to prepay your student loan.

L o a n   S n a p s h o t

$10K WILL GET YOU $125

For every $10,000 you borrow, you'll repay approximately $125 per month.

LOCATING INFORMATION ON YOUR STUDENT LOAN DEBT

There's no lack of places to go to find out information on *your* student loan debt. Try these for starters.

National Student Loan Data System (NSLDS). The main repository of government student loans. Call 800-4-FED-AID or go to http://www.nslds .ed.gov/.

Note: You'll need a PIN, or personal identification number, to access the site. If you don't have one from your student loan documents, go to https:// pin.ed.gov/request.htm and ask for one.

National Student Clearinghouse—Loan Locator. The Clearinghouse only accommodates borrowers of the Federal Family Education Loan Program (FFELP), but if that's you, it has a wealth of information on your loan. Find it at http://www.studentclearinghouse.org/secure_area/loan_locator.asp.

Note: Plug in your Social Security number and date of birth to find your loan information.

Credit Bureaus. Check the three major credit bureaus for data on your loan:

Equifax	Experian (formerly TRW)	TransUnion
P.O. Box 740241	P.O. Box 20022	Baldwin Place
Atlanta, GA 30374-0241	Allen, TX 75013	P.O. Box 1000
800-685-1111	888-EXPERIAN	Chester, PA 19022
http://www.equifax.com	888-397-3742	800-888-4213
	http://www.experian.com	http://www.tuc.com

How to Prove You Paid Off Your Loan

In the case of proving you have paid off your student loans, you need to contact the government agency that administered your loans or who oversaw the agency that administered your loans. In that case, that means contacting one or more of the following organizations:

- **National Banks.** Office of the Comptroller of the Currency, 1301 McKinney Street, Suite 3710, Houston, TX 77010, 800-613-6743, http://www.occ.treas.gov
- **Federal Savings and Loans.** Office of Thrift Supervision, 1700 G Street, N.W., 5th Floor, Washington, DC 20552, 800-842-6929, http://www.ots.treas.gov

WHAT DO YOU DO IF YOU'VE PAID OFF YOUR LOANS BUT YOUR LENDER SAYS YOU HAVEN'T?

This is an exasperating situation. You've paid off your loans, moved on with your life, and after three years or so, discarded your paperwork and documents saying that the loan obligation has been fulfilled. Then one day you open the mailbox and notice a letter from a collection agency looking for more money on your student loan. The letter says that, despite what you think, your loan *isn't* paid off.

I know it's exasperating because it happened to me, Brian O'Connell. I paid my loan. I tossed away my paperwork after three years. Then I got that letter from a collection agency saying they wanted more money. Worse, they're acting on behalf of the U.S. Department of Education, which administered my loan and sent me the letter acknowledging that the loan was paid off.

Now, I know what you're thinking. A government agency making a mistake like that? Impossible! But there it was. So, after flipping out and venting my anger on the collection agent over the phone (probably not the best move to make but I had to admit it made me feel better), here is what I had to do to solve the problem.

The position of the Department of Education and the collection agency was that the loan was never completely paid off. Worse, it was up to me to prove that it was—even though I had foolishly discarded the paperwork saying I had paid off the loan years ago. I hadn't kept any bank records, either.

The first move was to contact my bank and get a copy of my canceled checks. Banks do keep records of these transactions dating back six years or so. Some even keep records in computer databases or on microfiche longer than that. With the canceled checks as proof, the collection agency backed off and I never heard from them again.

But what if my bank had merged, consolidated, or just plain gone out of business? Then it gets tricky—you have to go to the next level.

- **Credit Unions.** National Credit Union Administration, 1775 Duke Street, Alexandria, VA 22314, 703-518-6300, http://www.ncua.gov
- **State Banks Members of the Federal Reserve System.** Board of Governors, Federal Reserve System, 20th and Constitution Avenues, N.W., Washington, DC 20551, 202-452-3693, http://www.federalreserve.gov
- **State Banks Not Members of the Federal Reserve System.** Federal Deposit Insurance Corporation, 550 17th Street, N.W., Washington, DC 20429, 800-934-3342, http://www.fdic.gov
- **The U.S. Department of Education.** Office of Postsecondary Education, 400 Maryland Avenue, S.W., Washington, DC 20202, 800-433-3243 (voice), http://www.ed.gov.

Short of canceled checks or legitimate paperwork, you have the following options to help prove you have paid off your loan:

Sworn affidavits. If a spouse or former roommate saw you write checks to pay off your student loan, then he or she can sign and you can issue a sworn statement testifying to that effect.

Old credit reports. Contact your credit report agency and see if they have old documents that show your loan is paid up.

Old IRS records. If you itemized the interest paid on your loan on your tax returns, the IRS should have that on record. Contact the IRS and ask for your records the year you paid off your loan and highlight interest rate deduction and send it to the collection agency.

Old school. Your former school should have received a note saying your loan was paid off from the agency or institution that issued the loan. Try your school's bursar's office or financial aid office.

The education ombudsman. Reach the U.S. Department of Education's ombudsman at 877-557-2575 or check out its Web site at http://www.sfahelp.ed.gov. The office specializes in loan disputes.

CHAPTER REVIEW

- Realize that you signed a promissory note on your loan and understand what it means.
- Familiarize yourself with your various loan repayment options.
- Know your loan payment schedule.
- Find out what to do if you've paid your loan, only your lender doesn't agree.

4

DEBT TRAGEDIES,
PAYMENT STRATEGIES

There are two schools of thought on debt repayment strategies. Some call the notion of debt management an art. Others call it a science. After five years as a trader on Wall Street and after ten years of writing about personal finance, I'd call it a mind-set.

You really have to be a pragmatist to tackle debt. It's a thankless, no-glamour task, akin to cleaning the gutters or undergoing a root canal. Burdensome responsibilities, yes, but necessary ones, too.

Like most matters in life, you have to set the table before you can eat. You have to lay the foundation and build a house before you can live in it and enjoy it. Same with retiring your student loan debt. It's dirty work that, once finished, lets you to go on and enjoy the by-products of that debt retirement—more money, less worries, and a sparkling credit rating that will enable you to buy that dream home or open that coffee shop downtown that you've always dreamed about. Those things—and not your stu-

dent loan debt—make life fulfilling. But you can't get to those fulfilling life goals without clearing away that debt first.

So imagine your mind-set when you graduate from college,
enjoy the accolades from your friends and family, and look for-
ward to embark on the rest of your life, diploma in hand and wind
at your back.

That euphoria exists only long enough until you get that first
student loan statement in the mail—the one with the eye-popping
$25,000 figure on it staring back at you from the bottom of your
statement.

Calgon, take me away, right?

Well, if you don't adopt that "can do" mind-set I referred to
previously, your student loan debt can become a student loan
problem faster than you can say, "Ah, I'll pay it next month."

That's why planning your loan repayment schedule around an
overall financial plan is so important. In Chapter 1, we touched
on the importance of managing credit card debt and establishing
a budget. But you also have to figure out how to channel that aggressive, bulldog mind-set into taking control over your financial
life and carving out a strategy for paying your student loan debt.

Let's tackle that issue right now.

THE COST OF HIGH DEBT

When you're talking about tackling your student loans, you're
really talking about avoiding lifestyle-crippling debt.

One of my favorite movies is *Apollo 13* with Tom Hanks, Kevin
Bacon, and Ed Harris. Fine actors, all, but it's Harris who has the
best line in the film. Faced with a potential catastrophe up in
space with a banged-up space capsule that might not survive reen-
try into the earth's atmosphere, Harris, as the NASA commander,
is the guy who has to solve the problem and bring the astronauts
home safely. Turning to his team, Harris gives them their march-
ing orders and says point-blank, "Remember, failure is not an option."

Failure is not an option. What a great concept for addressing your student loan debt. Why? Because the price for failing to pay off your student loan debt in a timely manner is a stiff one.

Let's look at reality. The more student loan debt you accumulate (and don't pay off), the tinier the mortgage you're likely to get when you buy a home. Or the smaller the loan you'll get to buy a new car. Or how about your career? Many companies now rely on credit reports to hone in on your character when you're applying for a job. If they see a heavy debt load, that's a big red flag. Hiring managers reason that if you're not reliable enough to pay your debts, you're not reliable enough to come work for them.

Face it. Debt gets expensive after a failed student loan payment effort and the ensuing nasty credit rating you'll get. That will impact everything that happens to you financially in life, from having to buy a smaller home—or heaven forbid, having to rent one because you don't qualify for a mortgage—to the amount of money you'll be able to put away for retirement. It won't be as much if you face a mountain of loan debt, meaning you could be spending your Golden Years working under the Golden Arches to make ends meet.

ESSENTIAL VERSUS NONESSENTIAL DEBT

As I've mentioned, not all debt is created equal. Okay, so it's not Thomas Jefferson, but humor me for a moment.

Some debts have more impact on your life than others. Those are the debts you need to square away first. Let's call that essential debt. Then there is the debt that, while serious, doesn't rise to the level of critical mass—the kind of debt that, if not handled properly, can cause your financial life to implode. Let's call that nonessential debt.

Obviously, essential debt is a priority and should be paid off first. Examples of essential debt are your rent or mortgage. If you don't pay that debt, you lose your home. I'd call that essential. Then there are your utility bills—your electricity, your heat, your water, or phone services. The loss of any one of them could lead to a life-threatening situation (for example, your house is on fire but you have no phone to call 911).

Child support is another essential. True, not too many post-collegiate Americans face child support, but if you do, you've got to pay it first. A judge could haul you off to jail if you don't. Car payments, too, might be considered essential debt, especially if you need to travel a significant distance to your job.

Then there is nonessential debt. Nonessential debt includes your credit card and student loan bills. Yes, I know. I've spent the better part of the book so far making my case for the importance of paying off your student loan debt and, to a lesser extent, your credit card debt.

But let's face facts. If you miss a student loan payment or two, or four or five, for that matter, your life isn't placed in jeopardy as it might be if you lose your home or utilities because you neglected those debts.

Still, while your student loan debt isn't at the essential level of your home or utility debt, it could be if you ignore it long enough. Yes, you can skate a while on your student loan debt without significant consequence. But let it go too long and you'll find creditors banging on your door and the IRS looking to garnish your wages. Then your student loan becomes essential debt faster than you can say "poorhouse."

FACING DEBT HEAD-ON

Job one for your student loan financial campaign is paying off your loan debt in the shortest amount of time. This keeps those crushing interest payments low and gets your loan out of the way so you can use your money for other endeavors. That means looking at your loan debt in unconventional ways. For example, I've noted that, with most student loans, you have a grace period after you graduate of up to nine months to begin paying off the loan.

At first blush, that seems like a real benefit. Whew! I don't have to deal with those monthly loan bills for almost a year!

But wait a minute. If you already have a good-paying job and can absorb the monthly financial hit, why not start paying off those loans *right now*? Why wait for nine months, thus extending your time line for getting out of student loan debt by nine months, and start taking care of business right now?

The answer is you don't have to wait. If, as I mentioned previously, job one is really getting out of debt as quickly as possible, why accept a grace period at all if you don't have to? Who needs an 8.25 percent interest rate hanging over his or her head any longer than he or she has to?

Also, why accept a graduated repayment? I know, I know. I mentioned it myself in Chapter 3. But that was only in the spirit of full disclosure. I wouldn't be doing my job if I didn't lay all the facts and all the options out in front of you.

But if paying off your debt as soon as possible is the goal, why string things along with a graduated loan repayment plan by which your payments start off small and then inch upward until you're done paying it off? The reality is that by accepting a smaller monthly bill now, you're really giving your lender permission to extend your loan payments further down the line and thus generate more interest. In other words, there's more of your money going into their pockets because you didn't want the burden of slightly higher payments early on. Better in my book to accept as high a payment level as you can and get the debt eliminated more quickly.

Think of graduated repayment plans as painting a house. With the graduated payments, you're essentially using a smaller but easier-to-use brush. True, the small brush might make the job easier to do up front, especially if you're not used to painting houses. But the bigger brush will get the house painted faster.

Okay, we're on a roll now. Here are some other ways to pay off your student loan debt faster. See if they don't make sense for your loan situation.

Be the early bird. Pay interest on your student loan while you're still in school. Granted, many of you reading this book are out of school, but for those who aren't, by paying your loan interest now, you can save thousands of dollars in accumulated interest down the road. (Think of interest on a loan as a snowball rolling down the hill, growing bigger and bigger the farther it goes.) For a total loan of $20,000, interest payments should only be about $20 per month. Start taking care of it now and save big bucks down the road.

All in the family. Why not ask your family members to help pay for school? Instead of a microwave oven or a set of golf clubs for your college graduation gift, ask for money to pay down your school debt. For example, maybe a few family members can pony up (collectively) $1,000 annually while you're still in school or for the first few years when you're out of it. For a loan of $1,000 at 7.66 percent over a 20-year time line, your total bill is $1,957. But over 10 years that bill slides down to $1,434. Big difference, especially when you're loan is likely higher than $1,000.

The incentive plan. I mentioned loan incentives in the last chapter, but they're worth mentioning again. Many lenders will reward regular payers or those who make automatic deduction payments with reduced interest rates. If you're paying regularly, or electronically, check with your lender to see if there's a rate cut in it for you. If they balk, demand one. Chances are, in the interest of good customer service and, with banks anyway, the prospect of a customer for life, they'll give it to you.

Embrace the 15 percent rule. By and large, your monthly student loan amount should be no more than 15 percent of your monthly salary. But if you can afford to, by all means pay more.

Get high first. No, not that kind of high. I mean get after your high-interest-rate debt first. Paying off your credit cards is a necessity, because they usually bring higher interest rates to the table than your student loan does. Credit card debt, as I said in Chapter 1, is a huge obstacle to financial freedom and a real roadblock to paying off your student loan debt. Still, it's debt that has to be addressed. So when push comes to shove, pay off your credit card debt first.

More than the minimum required. Pay more if you can. The more you pay—even $10 per month—the faster you'll pay off your student loan, and the faster you'll rid yourself of those onerous interest payments. Consider this: Simply by adding $100 a month to the $200 minimum on a $20,000 loan, you can retire that debt in six years instead of ten years.

Get help. If you feel overwhelmed by your student loan debt, or your overall debt, get help. Call a financial planner (the first session is usually free) or contact the Consumer Credit Counseling Session at 800-388-2227). To learn how to pay off your debt faster, contact an organization called Good Advice Press (at 800-255-0899). They offer an action plan to help people pay off debt quicker and easier. I'll delve more deeply into this issue in Chapter 7.

Keep tabs on your spending habits. If you don't know how much money is going out, then it's very difficult to create and sustain a debt reduction battle plan. You've got to know how much money you're spending. Solution: Create a spending spreadsheet (Microsoft Excel will do fine) that tracks all your recent tax stubs, outgoing checks, and credit card bills. Then separate your expenses into different categories, such as savings, rent, bills, insurance, food, utilities, entertainment, and miscellaneous, and track them in a notebook for two months. By then you'll have a good handle on what you're spending and can start the process of trimming some excess fat off your spending habits.

Keep ATM at arm's length. Try not to visit an ATM machine more than once a week. Get out of the habit of using your bank card and into the habit of making your money last longer.

Doing well by doing good. Remember the TV show *Northern Exposure?* In it, Rob Morrow played a young New York doctor who is sent by Uncle Sam to a small Alaskan town to practice medicine in exchange for relief on his medical school debt.

Nobody is asking you to pack up and move to Moosejaw, but you can defray some of your federal student loan expenses by taking on public or nonprofit jobs. For the short term, anyway. Such jobs are low-paying in low-income communities but many come equipped with loan-forgiveness attachments. Such programs are especially in need of doctors, nurses, schoolteachers, and lawyers.

According to the U.S. Department of Education, you can eliminate up to 100 percent of your student loan debt if you are a:

- Full-time teacher in an elementary or secondary school that serves students from low-income families
- Full-time special-education teacher
- Full-time provider of early-intervention services for the disabled
- Math, science, foreign languages, or bilingual education teacher or in other fields designated as teacher shortage areas
- Full-time employee for a public or nonprofit family services agency
- Full-time nurse or medical technician
- Full-time law enforcement or corrections officer
- Full-time staff member of the educational side of a Head Start program

For more information on such programs, visit the U.S. Department of Education's Web site (http://www.ed.gov) or the Mapping Your Future Web site (http://www.mapping-your-future

.org). Type in "loan forgiveness programs" on the "search" function at each site.

Overall, the big step toward paying off your student loan debt is to create a debt payment plan and set a goal to get out of debt by a specific date. Keep your time line to eliminating your student loan debt to ten years or under. But the faster the better.

L *o a n* **S** *n a p s h o t*

THE HIGH PRICE OF CREDIT CARD DEBT

The longer you procrastinate paying off your credit cards, the more interest you'll pay. For instance, if you make minimum payments on $2,327 in credit card debt, you will pay more than twice the original amount by the time you make your last payment—probably 20 years down the road.

CALCULATING YOUR
STUDENT LOAN DEBT

I realize that I harp on the "interest rate thing," but its importance cannot be underestimated. Simply put, interest rates are a bear financially. The more debt you accumulate, the more interest payments you pay. Remember, the very definition of interest rate is that it's the price you pay for borrowing someone else's money. It's the lender's profit margin. The higher the interest rate, the more money they make, and the happier they get—at your expense.

That's not all. Student loans, like most loans, are framed so that your early loan payments go primarily to paying off the interest—and not the principal (the amount of your loan)—on your loan. A true understanding of the principal and the interest you are actually paying on your debt will, I believe, lead you to deal with the problem and pay off the debt faster. Not knowing what your estimated payments on both principal and interest will be (akin to an ostrich sticking its head in the sand) is a losing proposition. When the numbers are right there in front of you in all of their glory, you're more apt to tackle the situation if you know what you are confronting. It's like walking into a dark room to find your car keys. You're best chance of finding them is to flick on the light.

Thus, knowing what your payments are is like shedding light on your situation. No longer in the dark, you can proceed accordingly and pay off that debt. People who don't want to know what their debt is and who refuse to turn on the light are the ones who have nothing but trouble paying off their student loan debts.

There's really only one way to figure out what you can expect to be paying and that's to calculate your student loan debt. Some lenders will gladly provide this information for you. But if not, fret not, it's easy to calculate your monthly loan payments.

Here's an example of how to do just that. Let's say you have a total student loan obligation of $5,000. Given a loan interest rate of 8.25 percent and a loan term of ten years, you'll have a monthly loan payment of $61.33 (and you'll have 120 months of those payments). Incidentally, I didn't complete this calculation with a pencil or a pen. I used one of the myriad student loan calculators on the Web to figure out your loan payments. In most cases, all you will need to get that information is your loan balance, your loan interest rate, your loan term, and your minimum monthly payment (almost always $50).

In this example, I used the calculator at FinAid.com to calculate the loan payment. (Find it at http://www.finaid.org/calcula tors/loanpayments.phtml.) You'll also get a tally of your cumulative payment amount ($7,358.92 in this example) and your total interest paid ($2,358.92).

A bonus: On the site FinAid.com, the loan calculator will also estimate what kind of annual income you'll need to be able to afford to pay for your loan ($7,358.92 in this example).

Other good loan calculators can be found at http://apps.col legeboard.com/fincalc/sla.html and http://www.wellsfargo.com /per/student/loans/tools/calculators.jhtml.

AVERAGE STARTING SALARIES

When calculating your student loan debt, it helps to know what you'll be making in your first postgraduate job. Here some figures to start with:

Position	Degree	Annual Salary
Accountant	BS	$39,397
	MS	43,272
Architect	March	32,540
Chemist	BS	29,620
College/university faculty	PhD	34,700
Computer analyst	BS	37,460
Computer programmer	BS	48,602
Dietitian	BS	23,860
Economist	BS	27,200
Electrical engineer	BS	41,740
	MA	57,200
	PhD	70,800
Financial manager	BS	45,000
Lawyer	JD	45,000
Mathematician	BS	37,300
	MA	42,000
	PhD	58,900
Newspaper reporter	BA	23,400
Nurse	BS	39,900
Physical therapist	BS	44,460
Psychologist	BS	20,600
	MA	31,200
	PhD	37,800
Public relations specialist	BS	35,100
Teacher	BA	25,700
Veterinarian	BS	35,900

Source: *Occupational Outlook Handbook,* U.S. Department of Labor Statistics, 2001.

ESTABLISHING A BUDGET

Once you know what your loan payments are, you can start crafting a strategy to pay them off. The first thing to do is to get a handle on your expenses and the amount of money you have coming in, and then build a budget that you adhere to in paying off your debt. A budget tells you where you stand, how much you can pay, and whether or not you can get ahead of your debt, so to speak, by paying more than you actually owe on your student loan.

Use the information and tips provided in Chapter 1 along with the budget planner in Figure 4.1 to plan your loan payments, along with the rest of your financial obligations.

L *o a n* **S** *n a p s h o t*

ARE YOU READY?

Roughly 33 percent of all recent college graduates are unprepared to make their first student loan payment, according to a survey by Collegiate Funding Services in Washington.

TAKE ADVANTAGE OF YOUR RELATIVE YOUTH

When you create a budget you're doing yourself a big favor. In fact, it amounts to more than you might think.

What do I mean by that? Well, creating a budget right out of college will make you realize a few things. First is that, in the case of most student loan borrowers, your age is your ally.

Most—but certainly not all—student loan recipients graduate while in their 20s. That's good news. From a time line standpoint, there's no better time to be in debt than when you are young, if for no other reason than you have more time to pay it off and more time, after that debt is retired, to start saving for yourself, your family (if you have one), and your future. Plus, having been a college student, you are probably accustomed to living frugally.

This is an important point. All things being equal, you're not likely to earn $100,000 a year right out of school on your first job.

FIGURE 4.1 *Budget Planner*

Estimated Income	Monthly Amount	Estimated Expenses	Monthly Amount
Income Sources		**Housing**	
• Net salary		• Rent/mortgage	
• Interest income		• Gas/electricity	
• Investment income		• Water	
• Family		• Telephone/cell phone	
• Other			
		Food	
Nontaxable Income		• Buying lunch at work	
• Temporary assistance for needy families		**Transportation**	
• Veterans benefits		• Car payment	
• Social Security		• Car insurance	
• Other		• Car repair	
		• Bus	
		• Subway	
		• Other	
		• Health	
		• Doctors	
		• Insurance	
		• Prescriptions	
		• Other	
		Dependent Care	
		• Child care	
		• Elder care	
		Personal/Miscellaneous	
		• Clothing	
		• Laundry	

Source: CollegeBoard.com.

So, if you can manage to extend that frugal collegiate mind-set a few years, you can take huge steps with the money you save to get out of debt, be it credit card debt or student loan debt (hopefully both).

Another advantage to being a younger borrower is that you have plenty of control over keeping living costs low. You can take in a roommate, ride the bus to work rather than buy a car (and put yourself more in debt), and even eat at Mom and Dad's (if you live close by) and thus cut down on your grocery bill. All the money you save by following such measures can go straight to your student loan debt, putting you one big step closer to financial solvency.

Some sacrifices must be made to embrace a frugal lifestyle. College graduates are as human as anyone else and want to spend those first beautiful paychecks on nights out clubbing, weekend road trips, and plush apartments and clothes. It's okay to do some of that, just don't go overboard. Certain people never understand that common sense is really hip. It helps you avoid the paycheck-to-paycheck existence that too many Americans lead, because they couldn't separate the terms *want* and *need* in their mind's eye.

Get what you need now, while you're young. When you're a bit older, and have more cash on hand, feel free to go after what you want. But if you go after what you want first, then you'll be stuck in that paycheck-to-paycheck merry-go-round in middle age, wondering if you'll have enough to even get what you need.

SHOULD I PAY OFF MY STUDENT LOANS OR INVEST?

A fair question. And given my Wall Street background, I do have a thought or two on the subject. Remember, it all comes down to interest rates. In this case it's a good idea to invest money if you can earn a higher interest rate than you are paying on your student loans. For example, if the interest rate on your student loans is 4 percent and you invest in a mutual fund that promises a higher return, then you will be netting a gain.

That said, there's no guarantee that your mutual fund will even earn 4 percent next year. Hell, it could lose 4 percent. That's why I favor paying off your debt first. The interest rate fees you kill by paying off the loan alone make that strategy a savvy move.

But I also come down on the side of practicality. If you insist on going the investor route, put the maximum you can in your company's 401(k) plan (or if you're self-employed a "solo" 401(k) that caters specifically to small business types). If your company has a 401(k) matching plan, it's crazy to turn down free money. Because your retirement plan distributions are tax-deferred and come out of your gross paycheck amount and not your net, you'll hardly notice the money is missing.

Then leave enough in your budget to pay your student loan.

(I'll provide much more information on combining student loan debt management and investing in your financial future in Chapter 8.)

S t u d e n t   L o a n   C a s e   S t u d y

SHOULD I PAY OFF MY STUDENT LOAN THROUGH MY RETIREMENT PLAN?

"I have to admit, I knew this was a bad idea, but I did it anyway." So says Joanne Atwell, a 30-year-old personal fitness instructor who used her IRA money from the health club she managed to pay off her defaulted student loan debt. "I was just thinking that it would be nice to pay off my student loan in one lump sum, but using my retirement plan is not the way to go."

How so? First of all, taking money from your IRA or 401(k) early (before age 59½) is not without consequence. Early withdrawals are subject to a 10 percent penalty by the IRS in addition to any income tax due on the withdrawal. That percentage might rise if there are additional fees and penalties charged by the IRS. Plus, your retirement plan accumulates tax-free and you really hate to break that momentum you're making on compound interest earned.

"I wound up losing a lot more than I gained by using my retirement fund to pay my student loans," Atwell adds. "I wish I knew then what I know now."

TAKE ADVANTAGE OF TAX LAW CHANGES

Another great way to cut your student loan repayment costs is to leverage the U.S. tax code to your advantage. That's right, Uncle Sam is offering you a tax break. Current tax law allows college graduates to deduct up to $2,500 a year in student loan interest, with no monthly limits (it was up to 60 months before 2002). You don't have to itemize to claim the student loan deduction. You do have to file Form 1040 or Form 1040A, and married couples have to file jointly. Ask an accountant or a tax specialist how much you can save with your student loan deduction. Or call the IRS Help Line at 800-829-1040 and ask about tax benefits for higher education or check out IRS publication 970, *Tax Benefits for Higher Education,* which you can find at the IRS Web site http://www.irs.org.

CHAPTER REVIEW

Because most student loans are offered with relatively low interest rates, it really makes no sense to ruin your financial future to pay off your student loan debt. Stay the course and leave the IRA alone.

- Know the difference between essential and nonessential debt.
- Calculate your total student loan debt and factor it into your lifestyle budget.
- Take advantage of tax breaks from paying off student loan debt.

5

WHAT TO DO WHEN YOU CAN'T PAY

Deferment, Forgiveness, Cancellation, and Discharge

Despite the best of intentions, debt can happen anyway. Consider the bar owner who proudly claimed, "I opened this saloon 15 years ago with $78 in my pocket. After years of hard work and sacrifice, look at me now. Today I'm $300,000 in debt."

All together now: *Not all debt is bad!*. Wealthy financiers such as Donald Trump, Warren Buffett, and Henry Ford all battled debt problems before they made their fortunes. As the old saying goes, "Show me a millionaire and I will show you a heavy borrower."

Debt only becomes a problem when you can't pay it off. With student loan debt, plenty of things can go wrong that leave you in the lurch and unable to contribute to your loan obligation. Being young and right out school, maybe you can't find a job yet. Or maybe you found one, but were laid off in one of those "last hired, first fired" scenarios. Common sense, specifically the lack of it, can come into play, too. Flush with your success at landing a good job, you blow off your student loan debt like an 8 AM anthropology class. Why? Because you've got other fish to fry: dating, clothes, getting a good apartment, dinners, movies, happy hours, parties. With all that hoopla surrounding you, it's easy to overlook that $10,000 loan that put you in the position to be enjoying all these perks in the first place.

And they are perks. Buying a new Hermes scarf or slurping down cosmopolitans at Trader Vic's are luxuries that, as a recent college graduate, you may or may not be able to afford. Paying your student loan debts offers nowhere near as many laughs as happy hour with the gang, but then, your student loans are no perk. They're an obligation. A responsibility. A fact of life.

Hey, I understand human nature. Given a choice between paying your monthly student loan bill or heading for a long weekend on the beach with your friends, the beach likely wins out more often than not. Granted, it's not an adult decision, but I understand opting for the beach because I've made the same decision myself.

But think about it. Too many of those kinds of self-gratifying "me first" decisions really add up to work against you. Remember, it's always better to keep a regular schedule and pay your loan bill each month. Retiring the loan ASAP is the goal. But missing a loan payment once in a while isn't going to kill you, it's just going to take much longer and make it that much harder and more expensive to pay off your loan. And if you miss too many payments, your loan could easily go into default.

So, if you have the money but still ignore your loan, you only have yourself to blame.

But if, despite the best of intentions, through circumstances beyond your control, you just can't cover your loan payments, that's another matter entirely. You're going to need help then.

That's what the next two chapters are all about—what to do when you can't pay your loan. Here, in Chapter 5, we'll discuss the ingredients that contribute to loan defaults and offer some ways to avoid that happening to you. In Chapter 6 we'll examine the issue of loan consolidation, one of the best ways to handle your debt problems before they get too far out of hand. Consolidations are so big and so popular that they deserve a chapter of their own.

But that's the next chapter. Let's keep our eyes on the prize here and begin examining the problem of nonpayment and default. Loan default is a relatively dark subject, but one you have to understand, if only to spur you to greater heights to avoid it.

Let's get rolling.

HOW WE GET INTO DEFAULT TROUBLE

More and more, the federal government and private lending institutions have had to bring in third-party collection agencies to force borrowers to pay their student loan bills. "Unfortunately, many recent graduates are accepting jobs below their income requirements due to a stagnant growth of business and job opportunities," says Gary Williams, a senior executive at ACA International, the Association of Credit and Collection Professionals, an agency that has collected more than $50 million for 450 colleges and universities across the nation. "Due to this and other acquired living costs, former students are having trouble completing their financial obligations to their institutions in a timely manner."

The ACA reports that in 2001, collection agencies recovered $780 million in delinquent debt for the Department of Education.

HOW MUCH DEBT DO GRADUATES ACCUMULATE?

More than half of private and public college graduates owe between $14,500 and $17,900 on their student loans. The average starting salary for a college grad's first job? $30,000.

College Time Line	Percent	Typical Range of Debt
Public 2-year	31%	$1,000–$5,000
Public 4-year	51	$5,000–$14,500
Private 4-year	55	$8,500–$17,900

That's a lot of blown-off student loans.

I believe the reason for borrowers to get into default situations is a lack of a real-world financial education. How to budget.

How to live on a limited income. How to avoid credit troubles. Those kinds of things.

One solution to the problem—an easy one in my book—is to tally up your income and your outflow and see where you are debt-wise. Another is to recognize how much debt is too much debt.

There are some big, hard-to-miss red flags that tell you you've accumulated too much debt. Here are a few signs that you just might have too much debt:

- If you haven't got more than $10 in your savings account and haven't made a deposit to savings in months, you just might have too much debt.
- If you're in the habit of postdating checks, you just might have too much debt.
- If you habitually pay bills late, you just might have too much debt.
- If you had to sell valuables, like a car, an old baseball card collection, or a family heirloom piece of jewelry, you just might have too much debt.
- If you habitually pay the minimum on your credit card statement, you just might have too much debt.
- If you've ever taken a cash advance on a credit card to pay off another bill, you just might have too much debt.
- If you're forever borrowing money from family and friends, you just might have too much debt.
- If it's early in the calendar year and you already have a cash "crisis," you just might have too much debt.
- If you're surprised by the amount of money you owe on your credit card, or the low amount of money you have in your bank account, you just might have too much debt.
- If you live from paycheck to paycheck, you just might have too much debt.

To figure out if you have too much debt, use one of the many loan repayment and income estimation calculators available on the Web. They'll help you calculate how much debt you have and how much you can afford to pay, and help you develop a budget or action plan to get out of debt. Two of the best are:

1. EDWISE (http://www.edwise.org)—UCLA's financial planning Web site
2. The Occupational Outlook Handbook (http://www.bls.gov/ocohome.htm)—a great site to calculate future income based on your college degree and the industry you plan to get into

THE "I JUST DIDN'T KNOW" FACTOR

Not knowing one's full financial situation is a chronic condition among our nation's younger Americans. According to State Public Interest Research Groups (SPIRG), in a study of 1,012 college students titled "Big Loans, Bigger Problems," eight out of ten college students underestimated how much debt they are taking on to pay for higher education. In fact, a whopping 78 percent of students underestimated the cost of their loans by an average of $4,846. SPIRG also discovered that college graduates, when it comes to estimated annual income, are wearing some serious rose-colored glasses. Survey respondents said they expected to make an average of $39,016, while the average income for recent college graduates is $27,000, according to the study.

PREVENTING STUDENT LOAN DEFAULT

What can you do to stay out of student loan default? Basically, the same themes I've been pounding home for four chapters now apply here as well—themes such as establishing a conservative budget and living within that budget. Also, getting rid of luxury items in your budget like an expensive car or a $5,500 living room set for that new plush apartment of yours. Eating out every night won't help, either.

Other action steps you can take include:

- Pay down your student loan debt early or pay more than you owe on your minimum monthly payments. Studies show that early payoffs help eliminate bank account–crippling interest payments for the life of the loan.
- Use the grace period to save up money for your student loan payments. The trick here is to forget that it's a grace period. Treat it as a "loan payment" period.
- Once you make a budget, live within that budget for at least one year before making any big purchases, like a home or a car. Such purchases can leave your carefully constructed budget way out of whack.
- Hire a financial advisor to help you out. For as little as $90, you can get a professional road map to pay off your loan and live within your budget. If you can't afford one, try contacting your local consumer credit office.
- Don't hesitate to contact your lending institution as soon as you begin to experience problems handling your student loan. They can help with payment plans and offer some new financing options.
- Make sure you keep all your paperwork. Keep copies of all documents, canceled checks, and every piece of paper you sign your name to.
- Keep your lending institution posted on your whereabouts. Let them know when you have a change of address or phone number, or if you change schools or change your enrollment status.
- Get help as soon as possible if you have any difficulty maintaining your student loan repayment arrangement.
- Keep your credit card in a desk drawer and out of your wallet. Credit card debt can really hamper your debt repayment efforts.
- Above all, come hell or high water, be sure you make loan payments on time.

FIGURE 5.1 *Payment Estimation Based on Loan Amount**

Amount Borrowed	Projected Monthly Payment	Sufficient Annual Income
$ 5,000	$ 61	$ 9,200
7,500	92	13,800
10,000	123	18,400
12,500	153	23,000
15,000	184	27,600
17,500	215	32,200
20,000	245	36,800

*Source: American Institutes for Research, assuming an interest rate of 8.25 percent and ten-year repayment plan.

HOW MUCH MONEY WILL YOU NEED TO PAY YOUR LOAN AND STAY OUT OF DEFAULT?

This is a tricky question. By and large, if you have a full-time job you'll have little trouble paying the minimum amount on your student loan debt every month—if, that is, you stay within your budget and control your spending.

But how much is really enough? As I've said, if you can make payments that amount to up to 15 percent of your annual income, you'll be just fine. That'll leave you plenty of money to live on.

Based on payments equal roughly to 8 percent of your annual income, some more specific guidelines for income and loan payments can be established (see Figure 5.1). If, for example, you have accumulated $10,000 in total school loans on graduation, then, based on the 8 percent figure, you'd need a salary of about $18,400 to make your loan payments and have some breathing room financially. In that instance, monthly payments of $123 would cover the loan amount in ten years.

DEFAULT
A Primer

Defaulting can happen to anyone who's either had a string of bad luck or who was simply caught unprepared. There's not too much you can do if you've lost your job or had a medical setback that prevents you from earning enough money to pay your student loans.

But, just as often, default happens to people who just don't take care of business. They either ignore their student loans or slough off and use their money for other things such as creature comforts and luxuries.

To that end, avoiding default is a decision you must make. Will I pay off my loans or not?

There's an old story attributed to former President Ronald Reagan. He tells of a shoemaker who was making a pair of shoes for him when he was a boy. The shoemaker asked if young Reagan wanted a round or a square toe. Reagan was unsure, so the cobbler told him to return in a day or two and let him know. A few days later the shoemaker saw Reagan on the street and asked him if he had made up his mind. But Reagan was still unsure. "Fine," said the cobbler, "your shoes will be ready tomorrow." When Reagan came to pick up the shoes, one had a round toe and one had a square toe. Said Reagan, years later, "Looking at those shoes taught me a lesson. If you don't make your own decisions, somebody else will make them for you."

In the case of student loan neglect, your loan institution, left to its own devices, will make this decision for you: Your loan is in default.

What does this mean? First, it's not good news. If you don't repay some of your student loan in a given time period—usually nine months—the loan holder will notify the guarantor and instruct them to purchase the loan back. When that happens, you are in default of your student loan. When nine months goes by without so much as a dime going to your student loan debt, and you make no effort to contact the lender, the lender reasonably assumes that you do not intend to honor the terms of your loan agreement and make the required payments when they are due.

When the guarantor purchases the loan from your lending institution, the loan obligation—your loan obligation—becomes their headache and they will immediately take steps to collect from you. Usually, the unpaid balance on the loan is accelerated, meaning that the guarantor wants *all* the money you borrowed (principal and interest) and they want it *now*.

Going into default is a disaster from a personal financial standpoint. The consequences alone should make your hair stand on end. For starters, defaulting on your student loans can hit you where it really hurts—in the wallet. Loan guarantors can, by law, stick you with an additional collection fee of 25 percent *beyond* the principal, interest, penalties, and other collection fees you originally owed. Plus, collection agencies (more on them shortly) can and do charge the loan guarantors an added fee of up to 28 percent of the disputed loan amount. That commission is passed on to—guess who? You! Thus, you have to repay not just the loan amount, but the collection charge and assorted commissions, too.

Other consequences of default include:

- You may be sued for the entire loan.
- Your credit rating will be demolished, making it virtually impossible for you to get a loan from another lending institution.
- Your federal and state tax refunds can be withheld and redirected toward your loan debt.
- You'll have a tough time getting a credit card.
- Your paycheck can be garnished, that is, portions of it taken away from you to pay off your loan debt.
- You can forget about getting any more student loans or financial aid. Default leaves you out of the aid-assistance loop.
- You may forfeit your privilege of joining a professional organization or obtaining a professional license.
- Your lousy credit rating becomes a big red flag to employers, who may opt out of hiring you based on character issues.

- You may face increased penalties and fees on your student loan, including court fees.
- You'll likely have the pleasure of dealing with a professional collection agency (receiving intrusive phone calls at home or on the job, threatening letters, etc.).

CRITERIA FOR DEFAULT

The good news is that, recently at least, student loan default rates are going down. According to the U.S. Department of Education, the national "cohort" default rate for 2001 was 5.4 percent, an all-time low, down 0.5 percent from the 2000 rate and 5.6 percent for 1999. The cohort default rate for fiscal year 2001 is the number of borrowers of federal loans who defaulted within 12 to 24 months after leaving postsecondary education.

Still, you can't be too comfortable and assume that a default situation can't happen to you. As usual, knowledge is power. The more you know about student loan defaults, the less likely you'll be caught unaware and find yourself in a default situation. In fact, you need to hit specific benchmarks before you can be declared in default.

You may be considered in default for any of the following reasons:

- You stop making payments on your loan, resulting in the loan being declared delinquent. If a delinquent loan is not paid in full within 30 days, your loan is considered in default.
- You stop making the regularly scheduled monthly payments when they are due. Once you miss six monthly payments, you are in default of the loan.
- You miss payments and fail to let your lender know why. Not making arrangements with the lending institution to repay your loan often leads to default.

BEHAVIOR, NOT BACKGROUND, KEY TO LOAN DEFAULTS

Keep making good grades and watch your chances of defaulting on your student loan diminish. That's the conclusion reached in a recent study by Texas Guaranteed, an Austin, Texas–based student-lending organization: "Although the study does not prove a direct cause-and-effect relationship between grades and students' ability to successfully repay their loans, the findings do suggest that anything that can improve college persistence and completion would probably decrease the likelihood of default. The results also indicate that borrowers are succeeding in student loan repayment largely without respect to their ethnicity, their parents' education levels, or their family income."

"We found that default behavior hinges more strongly on factors that are at least partially under the borrowers' control," said Matt Steiner, TG's senior research analyst. "These factors include whether the borrower graduates, how long he or she spends in college, and how well the borrower does in his or her coursework. In addition, these findings are consistent with one of the core principles of the student loan programs—student loans are worthwhile investments that borrowers will be able to repay, particularly when borrowers succeed in their programs of study."

The TG study examined the default behavior of 12,776 undergraduate borrowers from Texas A&M University in College Station.

GETTING OUT OF DEFAULT

Getting out of a default situation primarily depends on your ability to communicate well with your lender, and to demonstrate your renewed ability to pay your monthly loan bills. To get that process rolling, contact your lender and tell them that you are in loan default but want to make arrangements to resume paying off your loan. Happily, they will work out a loan payment schedule with you. If you manage to keep paying those loans under the new arrangement for one year, chances are you will have the scarlet *D* word unbranded from your forehead. Make sure you follow up with your credit agencies to ensure that the default has been lifted from your credit report.

L o a n S n a p s h o t

UNCLE SAM CAN HELP

The U.S. Department of Education Debt Collection Service publishes a guide called *Guide to Defaulted Student Loans* to help students repay their defaulted student loans. It includes information about:

- Repaying a defaulted student loan
- Loan consolidation
- Loan cancellation and discharge

Call 800-4-FED-AID (800-433-3243) or 800-621-3115 for a copy.

DEFERMENTS

Sometimes you hit a rough patch and you need a little time to pay your bills. In that instance, a deferment may be worth examining. With a deferment, your lender okays delaying the repayment of the principal of your loan for a predetermined period of time.

Interest on the loan may or may not accrue, depending on the type of loan you have. With Perkins or Stafford loans, no interest accrues during the deferment period because the federal government pays the interest. For unsubsidized loans or private loans, interest continues to accrue throughout the deferment period.

Note that you may be able to take a break on interest payments on any type of loan during a deferment by *capitalizing* the loan. That means adding the existing interest onto the loan principal and rolling it into one big ball of financial obligations for you. Paying interest on interest is no way to go through life.

Another word of warning on deferments. Don't assume that if you apply for a deferment that you'll get one. Try to continue making payments—as much as you can, anyway—while your application is being reviewed and processed. It's a short trip from assumed deferment to default, so take nothing for granted.

How do you get a deferment? Start by contacting your lending institution and ask for the appropriate application for your deferment. State your case clearly and explain why you think you might qualify for a deferment (see Figure 5.2). It's fine to do so over the phone but a letter may have more impact (and you won't leave out important criteria that you might in a verbal discussion). Make sure you follow up after your request for paperwork and get the name of the primary contact you'll be dealing with and file it away. That person may exert the most influence over your deferment situation.

L *o a n* **S** *n a p s h o t*

DEFERMENT EXAMPLES

Deferment situations usually apply to those individuals who are least able to afford paying their loans, including:

- Students still in undergraduate or graduate school (and likely not making much money)
- Sick or disabled students who are in recovery or who are undergoing a rehabilitation or disease treatment program
- Those who have suffered a job loss
- Those suffering from economic woes
- Parents with young children (in limited situations)

FIGURE 5.2 *Deferment Eligibility Requirements*

Deferment Eligibility Chart

Form	Deferment Type	Time Limit	Stafford and SLS Loans			PLUS Loans				Consolidation Loans	
			Pre 7/1/87 Borrower	New[1] Borrower 7/1/87 to 6/30/93	New[2] Borrower 7/1/93	Loans Before 8/15/83	Pre 7/1/87 Borrower	New[1] Borrower 7/1/87 to 6/30/93	New[2] Borrower 7/1/93	Borrower Consolidates Before 7/1/93[7]	New[2] Borrower 7/1/93
SCH	In-School: Full Time	None	•	•	•	•	•	•	•	•	•
	In-School: Half Time	None		•	•		•	•		•	•
EDU	Graduate Fellowship	None	•	•	•	•	•	•	•	•	•
	Rehabilitation Training	None	•	•	•	•	•	•	•	•	•
	Teacher Shortage	3 Years		•							
	Internship/Residency Training	2 Years	•	•		•					
TDIS	Temporary Total Disability[3]	3 Years	•	•	•	•	•	•		•	
PUB	Armed Forces or Public Health Services[4]	3 Years	•	•		•					
	National Oceanic and Atmospheric Administration Corps[4]	3 Years		•							
	Peace Corps, ACTION Program and Tax-Exempt Organization Volunteer	3 Years	•	•		•					
UNEM	Unemployment	2 Years	•	•		•	•	•		•	
	Unemployment	3 Years			•				•		•
PLWM	Parental Leave[5]	6 Months	•	•							
	Mother Entering/Reentering Work Force	1 Year		•							
HRD	Economic Hardship	3 Years			•				•		•
PLUS[6]	In-School: Full Time	None				•	•	•			
	In-School: Half Time	None				•	•	•			
	Rehabilitation Training	None				•	•	•			

[1] "New Borrower" 7/1/87 to 6/30/93: A borrower who, on the date the borrower signed the promissory note, has no outstanding balance on (1) a Stafford, SLS or PLUS loan first disbursed before July 1, 1987, for a period of enrollment beginning before July 1, 1987, or (2) a Federal Consolidation loan that repaid a loan first disbursed before July 1, 1987.

[2] "New Borrower" 7/1/93: A borrower who received a FFELP loan with a first disbursement on or after July 1, 1993. The borrower has no outstanding principal or interest balance on a FFELP loan as of July 1, 1993, or on the date the borrower obtains a loan on or after July 1, 1993. This includes a borrower who obtains a Federal Consolidation loan on or after July 1, 1993, if the borrower has no other outstanding FFELP loan when the Federal Consolidation loan was made.

[3] A deferment may be granted during periods when the borrower is temporarily totally disabled or during which the borrower is unable to secure employment because the borrower is caring for a dependent (including the borrower's spouse) who is temporarily totally disabled.

[4] Borrowers are eligible for a combined maximum of 3 years of deferment for service in NOAA, PHS, and Armed Forces.

[5] A parental leave deferment may be granted to a borrower in periods of no more than 6 months each time the borrower qualifies.

[6] Deferment for parent borrower during which the dependent student for whom the parent obtained a PLUS loan meets the deferment eligibility requirements.

[7] A borrower who received a Federal Consolidation loan that repaid a loan made before July 1, 1987, for a period of enrollment beginning before July 1, 1987, is eligible for in-school deferment only if the borrower attends school full time.

3/28/03

Source: Texas Guaranteed Student Loan Corporation.

FORBEARANCE

Here's another term you should become familiar with if you're having trouble paying off your student loans. Like deferment, *forbearance* is a mechanism designed to help if you need to either temporarily lower or postpone your student loan payments.

Forbearance is really for those folks who want to pay their loans but can't and who were unable to get a deferment on their loans. The application process isn't as onerous as the one for deferments, and the bureaucratic headaches that always seem to accompany deferments and loan discharges aren't as prevalent with forbearances. Again, however, it is completely up to the lending institution to determine whether you are awarded forbearance.

If you are approved, be prepared to continue paying interest on your loan. If you can't, the lender will simply add it to the ongoing loan bill and it will cost you even more money.

Forbearance is the loan holder's way of saying "We feel your pain." As long as you make a good faith effort to stay in contact with your lending institution and make your financial situation known to them, getting a forbearance shouldn't be a major problem. Note that the forbearance is temporary, usually awarded in 12-month stretches for no longer than 3 years.

Start by contacting your lender and asking for the right paperwork. Fill it out, send it back, and follow up. Write down the name of your contact and file it away. Ask for that person whenever you feel like you're getting the runaround from the lender.

BANKRUPTCY

Declaring bankruptcy is the last resort for flailing loan recipients and should be avoided at all costs. A major "severe hardship" obstacle must be cleared to even obtain a hearing on a bankruptcy. If you've been kidnapped by Bigfoot or beamed up to an alien mother ship, you still may not qualify for bankruptcy. It's

FORBEARANCE EXAMPLES

Typically, forbearance goes to individuals who are:

- Not able to pay their student loan bill because of ill health or other personal problems
- Involved in a medical or dental internship or residency

the third rail of personal finance—don't touch it or you'll be scarred for life.

If there is no other way out and you've consulted an attorney and a financial advisor, then you may have no alternative but to declare bankruptcy—only if you have no choice.

Note that a great deal of misinformation is available, especially with Internet hucksters and other scam artists who promise that bankruptcy will wipe your slate clean if you do business with them— probably for a hefty fee. That's just not so. Some debts, including student loans, cannot be simply "wiped clean." They will haunt you for life under bankruptcy. As soon as you regain financial solvency the lender has every right to go after you for their money. And they will, using your IRS tax returns as evidence you're making money again. That's public information and easily available to your lender.

Plus, your bankruptcy hurts in other ways. It will

- stay on your credit report for up to ten years,
- render it nearly impossible to get additional credit, and
- impact your ability to get a job.

So whatever advice you take from this book, steer clear of bankruptcy. It just isn't worth it.

STUDENT LOAN OMBUDSMAN

Newspapers have ombudsmen—impartial observers who act as intermediaries between readers and journalists. So why shouldn't college lending organizations? Chances are your school or former school has a student loan ombudsman who can step in and help you resolve loan problems. The goal is to find creative alternatives for borrowers who need help with their federal student loans.

To find out whom your ombudsman might be, visit the Federal Student Aid (FSA) ombudsman Web site at: http://ombudsman.ed.gov.

Or reach the U.S. Department of Education ombudsman office at:

877-557-2575
Office of the Ombudsman
U.S. Department of Education
4th Floor, UCP-3/MS 5144
830 First Street, N.E.
Washington, DC 20202

CANCELING YOUR LOANS

Want a free ride on your student loan? You practically have to die to do so. Lenders really want their money back and are loath to let you out of your loan obligations.

But, in special circumstances, you can cancel your student loan, or at least part of it. You may be able to cancel your student loan if:

- **You pass away.** If that unfortunate occurrence takes place, then your family or financial steward can cancel your student loan.
- **You are permanently disabled.** You can cancel your student loan if you can prove you are unable to work because of an injury or illness that is expected to continue indefinitely or result in your passing away. You'll need a letter from your physician describing your situation, and you probably won't get the loan canceled if, as they say in the health care insurance industry, you had a preexisting condition when you took out the loan.

- **You are a member of the armed forces.** God knows that we don't do enough for our fighting men and women, especially in this day and age. So who wouldn't approve of a loan cancellation or deferment for former students serving in the U.S. military, the National Oceanic and Atmospheric Corps, or the U.S. Public Health Service.
- **You teach in poor neighborhoods and communities or provide some community service.** If you teach in underserved or poor areas, you may be able to get your student loan either deferred or canceled outright. The same goes for teachers who help the disabled.
- **You were the subject of a trade school scam.** Trade schools are an iffy proposition and lenders know that. Some schools close, some offer diplomas that are fraudulent, and some slam their doors while you're still in school. If any of those cases apply to you, then you have a good chance of getting all your student loan obligation canceled.

DEALING WITH COLLECTION AGENCIES

There's an old saying that nothing improves a driver's skills than the sudden realization that his or her license has expired. So it goes for the student loan recipient who receives his or her first jolt from a collection agency looking for some student loan money.

Collection agencies are about as popular as root canals and parking tickets in American culture, but they're very effective in reclaiming some $700 million annually in defaulted student loan monies for college lending institutions. They charge anywhere from 25 percent to 30 percent for the service—money that is usually added to the recipient's loan amount by the guarantor. Federal law states that collection agencies may charge a reasonable fee—payable by the defaulting loan borrower—as well as other penalties such as late fees and administrative fees. Obviously, your typical collection agent isn't spending the money on charm school. No, an agent's job is to act as a bulldog and sink his or her teeth into your ankle and not let go until you pony up the defaulted student loan dough.

There's not much you can do to fight the collection agency fees on your defaulted student loans. You can ask the agency to itemize their costs related to those fees, but don't expect much in response. There really isn't any law that can force them to do so.

But, as one wag said, you should have thought about that before you defaulted on your student loan.

L *o a n* **S** *n a p s h o t*

THE 40 PERCENT DILEMMA

According to the U.S. government, "first" collection efforts by agencies cannot result in fees of more than 30 percent of your student loan amount in question. "Second" effort fees can rise up to 40 percent. If you can manage to repay the loan amount to a collection agency within 60 days, the agency fees are usually waived.

SOME GOOD NEWS

Let's end the chapter on a high note. If you think default is a bummer to read about, try writing about it. *¡Ay caramba!* It's a real migraine.

So how about some good news? Here's what can happen if you keep up with your college student loans:

- **Solid credit.** Your regular payments on your student loans are noted on your credit reports. Regular payments equal good credit.
- **Lower finance charges.** When you make your loan payments on time, you're cutting the interest payments on your loan.

For example, when you make payments every 30 days, as opposed to every 40 days, fewer of your dollars go to interest and more go to principal. The end result? Your loan gets paid off sooner.

- **No collection agencies.** By staying ahead of the curve on your student loan, you keep the nasty collection agencies out of your life.
- **Lender discounts.** As I pointed out earlier, many lending institutions currently offer interest rate discounts to borrowers who make their payments consistently on time.
- **You're done.** You'll pay off your loan a lot quicker. Isn't that the point?

L o a n   S n a p s h o t

ACTION STEPS IF YOU'RE IN LOAN DEFAULT

- Pay your account in full with one lump sum.
- Establish satisfactory payment arrangements with your guaranty agency or collection agency (and possibly rehabilitate your loan).
- Consolidate your account into one new loan with new terms.

CHAPTER REVIEW

- Know how default happens.
- Work on ways to prevent default.
- Consider deferment or forbearance if you can't pay.
- Avoid bankruptcy at all costs.

OVERCOMING DEFAULT

"You know, you have to take responsibility over your own life, and I didn't do that with my student loans," says Dan Bradley, a 28-year-old unemployed physical therapist. "I only had myself to blame."

Bradley was 25 when he lost his job and soon his life went into a deep tailspin. "I couldn't find another job, couldn't make my car payments or my student loan payments. I had to borrow money from my parents just to keep my apartment."

After ignoring his student loan lender and their monthly bills, Bradley got a wake-up call in the form of a phone call from a collection agency. "That blew my mind," he says. "They were pretty nasty and aggressive about my loan."

Bradley finally called his school's financial office and they recommended he try to get either a deferment or a forbearance on his loan. "I called the lender and explained my situation and they sent me an application," he says. "I filled it out and a few weeks later I got a letter saying I could take some time off from paying my loan. It was a huge relief."

One year later Bradley had found a new job at a physical therapy clinic and had resumed paying his student loans. "This time I didn't take any chances—I paid $50 more than I owed every month, just to stay ahead of the game."

6

DEBT MANAGEMENT 101

Anatomy of a Loan Consolidation

Managing debt is like being back in school. You're always learning something. Specifically, you are always learning from your mistakes.

That reminds me of a story about a man whose wife had died. As the mourners were on their way to the cemetery, one of the pallbearers tripped over a rock. This jolted the casket and revived the woman, who was only in a coma. She lived another seven years and then one day really died. On the way to the cemetery again, the mourners approached the same spot. As they did so, the husband shouted out to the pallbearers, "Watch out for that rock!"

Learning from the past is a big part of managing debt. You're going to make mistakes, maybe miss some payments, and undergo some trial and error before you iron out the wrinkles in your student loan repayment campaign.

One of the great facets of debt management in this country is that you can usually get a second chance to correct your mistakes. As we saw in Chapter 5, you can delay your payments, extend your payments, or get them canceled altogether if things didn't turn out the way you wanted the first time around.

Another great way to minimize past student loan repayment miscues is to consolidate your student loans—the subject matter for Chapter 6. This is a viable option that offers you immediate financial relief if the debt burden you're under is too much to bear. Of course, in this era of relatively lower interest rates, "refinancing" your student loan might make even more sense.

So, loan consolidations. A good deal or not? Let's find out for sure.

WHAT IS LOAN CONSOLIDATION?

Think of consolidating your student loans as reorganizing all your key business contacts and putting them into one Blackberry or one Rolodex. Or think of it as combining your DVD remote, your stereo remote, your VCR remote, and your satellite TV remote all into one easy-to-handle device.

Imagine that? Bundling all your debt into one loan with one bill and one payment—maybe even with a lower interest rate. It's no wonder that loan consolidation is considered by many to be an organizational wonder for the 21st century.

By consolidating, you're actually lowering your monthly loan payments past the average ten-year student loan limit. The downside is that you're shelling out more money in interest payments because you will be making loan payments over a greater length of time. That's a big downside.

Student loan consolidations haven't been around that long, but they're certainly gaining visibility among the borrowing set. Despite popular myth, federal consolidation loans were not established to provide student loan borrowers with the ability to refinance their loans. Instead, loan consolidations were originally introduced by Congress to help borrowers simplify their loans and give them a shot at making lower payments if they were having trouble paying off their loans.

IS IT FOR ME?

Should you consolidate your student loans? It depends on what your financial situation is and what your financial goals are.

If your goal is immediate financial liquidity, that is, more money in your pocket for the short term, then consolidating may be a good way to go. But if your goal is to get rid of your student loan debt ASAP and you can manage those regular monthly payments, then it's not such a great idea, unless you can consolidate your loans with a bargain-basement interest rate that's much lower than the one you have now. Remember my mantra for this book: The sooner you pay off your loan, the more money you save and the better your financial health will be.

L *o a n* **S** *n a p s h o t*

REPAYMENT TIP

The optimal strategy for repaying a consolidation loan is to continue making the same payments you were making before you consolidated your loan, applying the extra amount to the principal.

DO I HAVE OTHER OPTIONS?

It's easy to jump right in and consolidate your student loans without thinking the whole thing through. One loan, one payment, maybe a lower interest rate. What's not to like, right?

There are, however, reasons not to consolidate your loans (I'll get into those shortly). That's especially true if you have other, better options available to you. Consider these scenarios:

- **I need a lower monthly payment.** Most lenders will be happy to discuss different loan repayment options, such as the graduated payment and income-sensitive payment plans discussed in Chapter 4.

- **I'm having trouble keeping up with my loan payments.** You can temporarily stop paying your loans, or at least reduce them, under either a deferment or a forbearance plan.
- **I just want all my loans rolled into one.** Your lending institution may be willing to purchase all your other student loans and bundle them together under one "roof." In financial circles, that's known as *loan serialization.*

WHAT AMERICANS OWE

- Average remaining student loan balance (men, 21–34): $12,900
- Average monthly payment (men, 21–34): $222
- Average remaining student loan balance (women, 21–34): $10,300
- Average monthly payment (women, 21–34): $141

Source: Collegiate Funding Services Survey.

WHAT ARE THE BENEFITS AND THE DRAWBACKS OF CONSOLIDATION?

I've already mentioned some advantages to consolidating your student loan. Immediate debt relief, potentially lower interest rates, and the simplicity of managing just one loan should be on that list (see Figure 6.1 for more pros of consolidation).

The primary drawback is that by consolidating your student loan, you are taking your original goal of paying off the loan as fast as possible right off the table. With the longer repayment timetable that comes with consolidated loans, comes more interest payments to make. Imagine paying for your college loan as your oldest child jets off to college for the first time. Unfortunately, that's a common occurrence for those who choose to consolidate their student loans (also see Figure 6.1 for more cons of consolidating your loans).

FIGURE 6.1 *Pros and Cons of Consolidation*

Pros

- **Fixed interest rates.** Unlike your traditional student loan with an interest rate that is variable throughout the repayment period (meaning it can move up and increase your loan payments), consolidated loans offer only fixed interest rates.
- **Immediate debt relief.** Your monthly loan payments will decrease as soon as you consolidate your loan.
- **Easy payments.** With loan consolidation, you make one monthly payment to one lender.
- **The incentives.** By consolidating, you can grab interest rate discounts of 1 percent for making 48 months of payments on time and .25 percent for choosing automatic debit from your bank account. This is standard procedure for most lending institutions.
- **Prepayment.** You can pay off your loan early with no penalty.

Cons

- **Increased costs.** Your loan costs will increase because of your loan's new extended repayment terms.
- **No deferment.** You may lose the privilege of deferment.
- **No cancellation.** You may lose the privilege of canceling your student loan.
- **Fixed rates.** If interest rates decline, good luck, you're stuck with the fixed rate on your loan.
- **No grace period.** There is no grace period for a consolidated loan. You have to start paying it right away.

Additional Benefits of Consolidating

Some other points on student loan consolidations include:

Incentive plans. Like traditional student loan plans, consolidation plans reward those borrowers who pay on time and on a regular basis. Under Sallie Mae's student loan consolidation plan, for example, you can save .25 percent off your interest rate by paying through automatic payroll deduction. Similarly, if you have more than $10,000 in loans and pay every month for four years, Sallie Mae will knock a full 1 percent off your loan's interest rate.

Tax-deductible. Consolidated student loan plans are tax-deductible in the eyes of Uncle Sam. The IRS enables student loan borrowers to deduct up to $2,500 in interest payments annually (as long as the borrower's gross annual income is below $100,000 for married couples who file together and under $50,000 for singletons).

ELIGIBILITY REQUIREMENTS

As long as you either are in a loan grace period or have already commenced paying off your student loans, you're eligible for a loan consolidation. If you are in default of your student loan, you have to work out a repayment plan with your current lender or agree to pay the financial institution that will distribute your consolidated loan on some type of income-sensitive loan repayment option.

You cannot consolidate your student loans if you are still in college, unless you are enrolled as a part-time student. You can, however, team up with your spouse if you are married and consolidate your student loans. Note that if you do so and one of you fails to pay his or her fair share of the loan, the lending institution will expect the other spouse to pick up the loan payment obligations.

WHAT CONSOLIDATION
CAN DO FOR YOU
My Take

Basically, loan consolidation simplifies your financial life for the short term. In exchange for lower immediate payment relief you agree to pay more over the longer extended loan payment periods that come with loan consolidation.

Loan consolidation enables you to funnel all your existing, outstanding student loans into one individual loan with one monthly payment. The loan gives you a new (hopefully lower) fixed-income payment structure, new loan payment terms, and a repayment timetable that can stretch out to 30 years. When the lending institution disburses your consolidation loan, it also pays off the outstanding balances of all your previous student loans.

The good news is that loan consolidation can help you lower your monthly loan payments, a big benefit if you're struggling to make ends meet or suffering under some other financial duress. How? By extending your repayment period from the traditional

10-year loan up to a 30-year loan. That frees up cash for you in the short term, on a monthly basis, to address other financial needs.

The bad news is that with consolidated loans, you wind up paying more in the long run for the privilege of refinancing your student loan. That's because of the "stretch factor"—when the lender moves your 10-year loan out to a 30-year loan. When that happens, the interest you pay on the loan can rise dramatically.

For example, let's say you have a $50,000 traditional 10-year Stafford loan. By consolidating your loan, you will likely get a break on the monthly payments, depending on the new interest rate, but you'll owe more over the life of the loan. How much more? In this instance, by extending the loan from 10 years to 30 years, you would owe $86,558 instead of the original amount plus interest accrued of $66,582 on a 10-year Stafford loan. Yes, you can prepay the loan and/or pay more than the monthly minimum amount required and cut that $20,000 or so gap down to size, but if you don't, you've just added $20,000 to your original loan amount by consolidating. By consolidating your loans, you are essentially taking your original loan and breaking them down into smaller pieces—pieces of which you'll be paying off in lower amounts but over a longer term than your original loans. That said, interest rates, which have been declining significantly in recent years, can potentially minimize any hike you see in your total student loan amount by consolidating it. More on that shortly.

WHO OFFERS STUDENT LOAN CONSOLIDATION PROGRAMS?

That depends on whether you have a government (or federal) student loan or a private one. Government loans can be consolidated through any government-approved private lending institution or through the U.S. Department of Education.

By and large, federal student loan consolidations are pretty easy to get. They're offered by just about every major federal loan organization, including the Federal Family Education Loan Program (Stafford, PLUS, and SLS), FISL, Perkins, Health Professional Student Loans, NSL, HEAL, Guaranteed Student Loans, and Direct Loans. Some banks and other private lenders offer consolidated loans for their borrowers as well. But get ready, you'll soon find yourself in negotiation over term rates. Remember that banks and other private lenders are businesses, after all, and will try to wheedle out every dime they can from you.

FEDERAL LOANS ELIGIBLE FOR CONSOLIDATION

Here's a list of organizations that offer student loan consolidation packages:

- Federal Stafford Loan (subsidized and unsubsidized)
- Federal Direct Loan
- Federal Perkins Loan
- Health Professions Student Loan (HPSL)
- Loan for Disadvantaged Students (LDS)
- Health Education Assistance Loan (HEAL)
- Nursing Student Loan
- Federal Insured Student Loan (FISL)
- Auxiliary Loan to Assist Students (ALAS)
- Federal Supplemental Loan for Students (SLS)
- National Direct Student Loan (NDSL)
- Federal Parent Loans for Undergraduate Students (PLUS)

WHAT'S THE BIG DEAL ABOUT INTEREST RATES?

I previously mentioned a new interest rate for loan consolidations—for good reason. In most instances, consolidated loans allow harried borrowers who have fallen behind paying back their student loans to reorganize their loans into one package. A new lease on your student loan life, if you will. But you can get a break on your interest rates, too, by consolidating, and that can mean real out-of-pocket savings for you.

Here's the deal. Interest rates on consolidated student loans are fixed, meaning they can't and won't change. The rate you get the day you consolidate your loans is the rate you have the day you pay off your consolidation loan. To make things even sweeter, Congress made sure that the fixed interest rate on student loan consolidations could never exceed 8.25 percent.

But traditional student loan interest rates vary. They could be 5 percent or 6 percent or whatever, depending on whom you're dealing with. But historically, student loan interest rates have edged closer to that 8.25 percent mark rather than farther away. In the past few years, however, student loan rates have trended downward (along with most other loan interest rates). By 2003, student loan interest rates were hovering at about 3.5 percent. That's a big savings over a loan based on an 8.25 percent rate. For example, a loan recipient who borrows $20,000 for 10 years at 3.42 percent will pay roughly $5,400 in interest. But a student borrower operating under a loan with an 8.25 percent interest rate, under the same time line and dollar amount, would pay about $9,200 in interest rates.

Of course, if you lock in what you consider a good rate, and interest rates go down even further, you're pretty much stuck with the interest rate you signed on for. But with interest rates at historic lows so far in the 2000s, there is a bit less to worry about on that front.

L *o a n* **S** *n a p s h o t*

INTEREST RATE FACTS

Most traditional student loans are offered with varying interest rates. These rates are tied to U.S. Treasury bill rates. As an ex–Wall Street bond trader, I can tell you that where Treasuries go, interest rates follow. The good news is that in July of 2002, new student loan interest rates took effect that saw rates decline from 4.06 percent to 3.42 percent. That .64 percent decline in interest rates can significantly reduce the amount of money you'll pay on your total student loan.

HOW DO I APPLY?

Applying for a consolidated loan is cheap and easy. Just contact the loan institution and be ready to provide the information in Figure 6.2.

After you apply for your consolidated loan, the following things will happen:

- Your lending institution may need to contact you to verify your account or application information, so be sure to include your phone number or e-mail address on your application.
- Your lender will ship out a confirmation kit with copies of all your loan documents and paperwork.
- Take time to review all this information. Make sure everything is accurate. Go ahead and make changes if necessary. Once you approve the loan application, sign and return it to your lending institution.

FIGURE 6.2 *Information Needed to Consolidate Your Student Loans*

Contact Information

Name _____

Current address _____

Social Security number _____

Date of birth _____

Home phone number _____

Driver's license number _____

State driver's license issues _____

Employment Information

Your employer name _____

Employer address _____

Employer phone _____

School Information

Date of graduation or date of leaving school _____

Name of school _____

References

Name and address (parents, teachers, employers okay) _____

Name and address _____

Student Loans Being Consolidated

Loan type _____

Loan balance and rate _____

Loan holder information _____

- Your lender will then verify that the information you presented on your application is true. That usually means checking with credit report agencies, other lenders, and your school's financial department.

If everything checks out, your consolidated loan will be approved. You will receive notification from your lender, with feedback on your new loan and payment terms.

All told, the entire loan consolidation process can take from four to eight weeks to complete. Once approved, repayment begins immediately, with the first payment due within 60 days.

L *o a n* **S** *n a p s h o t*

NO REFUSAL

Don't allow your lending institution to get away with rejecting your loan consolidation request for any of the following reasons. By law they can't.

Your lender cannot refuse to consolidate your student loans because of:

- The amount of loans you wish to consolidate
- The school you attended
- The new interest rate charged on a consolidation loan
- The types of repayment schedules

Also note that a federal consolidation loan comes with:

- No credit check required
- No qualifying criteria except your student status
- No cosigners
- No cost or fees when you apply
- No employment check
- No prepayment penalties

WHAT ARE MY REPAYMENT OPTIONS?

Overall, your repayment terms on your consolidated loan aren't too much different from the terms on your original student loan or loans.

Level repayment—the vanilla approach. "Level" means you pay equal monthly payments over the life of your loan.

Graduated repayment plan I. A unique repayment option that allows for interest-only payments for the first one-third of your total repayment period. After that, level monthly payments are required for the remaining two-thirds of your repayment period.

Graduated repayment plan II. Same idea as with the previously mentioned plan but only on a quarterly basis. This plan only requires you to pay interest for the first quarter of the repayment period. For the second quarter, you pay level monthly payments. Your lender will revisit the terms with you during the last half of your loan, enabling you to choose the option that works best for you.

Income-sensitive repayment plan. This is similar to the income-sensitive repayment plan we covered in Chapter 3. Here you pay equal monthly payments. After you are in repayment, your monthly amount can be adjusted if your financial situation takes a turn for the worst.

Extended plan. If you have a bundle of loan money to pay off, you can get an extended loan that gives you more time to do so. Typically, the cutoff line is $30,000 or more. Payments, which may be level or graduated, can extend to 25 years if needed. Note that interest rate payments extend with them.

Length of Repayment Period

You can pretty much calculate the term of your consolidated student loan before you even apply for one. Based on lending industry figures, Figure 6.3 shows how long you can expect your loan repayment period to be, based on your total outstanding student loan debt.

FIGURE 6.3 *Consolidation Repayment Chart*

Repayment Periods
Less than $7,500—10 years
$7,500–$9,999.99—12 years
$10,000–$19,999.99—15 years
$20,000–$39,999.99—20 years
$40,000–$59,999.99—25 years
$60,000 and above—30 years

LAST-MINUTE TIPS

Let's end the chapter with some last-minute tips on consolidating your student loans—just so we don't miss anything.

Tax-deductibility. By and large, loan consolidations are tax-deductible. Borrowers who meet eligibility requirements may deduct all or some of their student loan interest. Please consult your tax professional before taking any deductions.

A consolidation combo? You can't combine public and private student loans. By law, federal loans and private loans must be separate.

Grace periods. While you can and maybe should (depending on your financial circumstances) consolidate your loan during your grace period, you will lose that grace period once your application for a new bundled loan is approved.

Consolidating PLUS and federal Stafford loans. You can consolidate PLUS and Stafford loans as long as you use the same Social Security number.

Be prepared to pay a minimum. Lending institutions may insist on a minimum loan amount to make it worthwhile for them to handle your loan. The amount varies from lender to lender and you can try to negotiate that amount.

A TALE OF TWO CHARTS

Grace periods do matter when consolidating your student loans. Usually, you can save big on interest payments by consolidating *during* your grace period than *after.* That's because lending institutions typically offer better interest rates if you consolidate during the grace period. Following are charts from Sallie Mae, showing repayment schedules for loans consolidated during and after the student loan grace period expires. As you can see, the borrower with $50,000 in loan debts would have saved $5,120 in interest by consolidating during the loan period.

Consolidation *during* Grace Period at 3.5 Percent

Initial Repayment Balance	Monthly Payment	Total Payments
$ 10,000	$ 71	$ 12,868
20,000	116	27,838
30,000	174	41,757
40,000	200	60,075
50,000	250	75,094
75,000	337	121,242
100,000	449	161,656

Consolidating *after* Grace Period at 4.125 Percent

Initial Repayment Balance	Monthly Payment	Total Payments
$ 10,000	$ 75	$ 13,427
20,000	123	29,404
30,000	184	44,106
40,000	214	64,172
50,000	267	80,214
75,000	363	130,855
100,000	485	174,474

Source: Sallie Mae.

Default? Not a deal breaker. In most cases, defaulted loans can still be consolidated. However, you have to be repaying your loan, with at least three consecutive payments under your belt, or have agreed to pay your new consolidated loan under some type of graduated repayment plan process. Sorry, bankruptcy doesn't apply. Once the courts get involved, lending institutions tend to stay away.

WHEN GOOD CONSOLIDATIONS GO BAD

When Larry Hawes decided to consolidate his student loans—he had four of them—it really made sense.

"I would be getting one bill, making one payment, and my interest rate would be lower," he says. "To me, that's a great deal."

What Hawes didn't realize is that, even with the four loans, he had been making payments on time and for four years straight. He had already seen the lender knock down his interest rate on the loan by one percentage point and he was only two years away from finishing off the loan.

"I did it for simplicity sake and to get a better interest rate," he says. "In the end, I got neither."

CHAPTER REVIEW

- Know the ins and outs of loan consolidations.
- Decide if consolidation is right for you.
- Try other options—like renegotiating interest rates with your lender—first.
- Don't be lured by easy interest rates. Your loan amount will grow and lower rates won't make up the difference.
- Pay on time and avoid the need to consolidate altogether.

7

DEBT MANAGEMENT

Do It Yourself or Go to a Pro?

There's an old saying about the perils of debt. To get back on your feet, just miss two car payments. Like most examples of dark humor, there's a slice of truth to it. If, after all, you do miss a few car payments, pretty soon you will find yourself out of the driver's seat and back pounding the payment.

That's how it goes when you can't meet your financial obligations. Businesses that gave you the money in the first place to buy things *can and will* take away those same things from you. In the student loan world, financial institutions can't take away your diploma and they can't take away your college education. What they can take away is your credit rating and your good name, which is just as bad as taking your name or your sheepskin in my book. In the financial world, if you don't have credit, then you pretty much cease to exist to lenders and creditors.

Fair or unfair, that's the way it is. The thrust of this book has been to pay off your debts as soon as possible and avoid any dates with default forms or debt collectors. Sometimes, as we've seen, that isn't always possible. You lose a job or get sick and the next thing you know you're fielding calls from obnoxious collection agency reps who don't see a human being on the other end of the phone line. Instead they see a commission check.

Tough to make any headway in your life under those conditions. But that's what debt can do to you if you can't control it. In the process of researching and writing this book, I began looking at debt as a catch-22 situation. Specifically, the key to avoiding debt is to see the hard times coming and take action steps to rectify the situation—to nip any problems in the bud before they blossom and bite you on the nose. Of course, if you could see tough economic times coming, you could junk your job, move to Las Vegas, and make a good living at the blackjack or roulette tables seeing things happen before they occur.

As appealing as that might sound, it's not realistic. Sometimes, through self-destructive financial habits or through loss of a job and income, you have to wrestle with debt anyway. And get yourself out of debt.

That's what I want to talk about in Chapter 7—handling debt management problems, either on your own or through the help of a professional debt counselor. By debt management, I mean handling your credit and lender obligations so your financial health is pristine and pure. That means creating an overall debt management framework where you not only pay off your student loan debts, but also learn how to manage your entire debt situation in the process—for life.

If you're disciplined and financially savvy, you'll probably never have to worry about debt management problems. But if you make mistakes or run a gauntlet of bad luck and don't make it out the other side intact, it's just plain smart business to know what steps to take if you're buried under an avalanche of debt.

In the previous two chapters, I spelled out how things such as default and loan consolidation can help get you through tough times—until you can get back on your feet. Let's widen the scope and talk about how problems, not just with your student loan but with all of your financial obligations, can leave you in the lurch, financially at least. In that case it's best to have a blueprint on understanding the red flags that signal problems on the horizon, dealing with creditors, and the pros and cons of getting professional debt counseling help.

Again, I hope it never comes to that. But if severe debt happens, it's always better to confront it and handle it than to ignore. In many cases, that's how debt sufferers get into their unfortunate positions in the first place.

Let's get going.

RECOGNIZING THE RED FLAGS THAT LEAD TO DEBT

When you're paying off your student loans, or paying off any debt for that matter, it's a great idea to know where you stand financially. Specifically, it's a great idea to recognize any warning signs that might foretell a personal economic plunge that may take years to recover from. For example, in the student loan repayment realm, three unopened invoices from your lender lying in a pile on your desk is a big red flag that you're not keeping up with your loan payments.

Here are some common financial red flags to look for in your busy life:

- **Your bank account is consistently overdrawn.** If you keep getting those thin envelopes in the mail from your bank telling you that your checking account is overdrawn, it's time to regroup and find out why you're not keeping up. Tip: Ask your bank for overdraw protection against your checking account. For a few bucks each month, most banks will be happy to comply.
- **You are only able to make the minimum monthly payments on your credit cards.** A biggie. If you can't maintain a clean credit card bill each month then you're staring at big trouble down the road. At 15 percent or so interest, credit

card companies clean up when you pay only the bare mini-mum of your monthly bill. At those rates, that new jacket you bought for $80 three months ago can cost you $350 in a few months if you don't pay your credit card bill in full. Tip: If you have multiple credit cards, cut all of them up save one. And use that only for emergencies.

- **You and your partner, if you have one, are arguing about money.** Money is an emotional issue, a power struggle some-times between couples who usually have different ideas of how cash should be handled. If you and your spouse or part-ner are haggling over bills more than usual, it's probably be-cause your bills are higher than usual. Tip: Agree on a budget and a spending allowance, if necessary, then stick to it.

- **Your savings account is busted.** Money experts agree that a savings reserve of six months of your annual salary is man-datory to ride out rough economic times, like the loss of a job or a serious illness. If you don't have any money at all in your savings account, it's time to reexamine your budget and see where your money is going every month. Tip: When you get paid, pay yourself first; take 10 percent of your check and stash it in a savings or money market account.

- **You are juggling your monthly bill payments.** If you're ap-plying selective reasoning to your monthly bill payments ("Hmmm, we'll pay the phone bill this month, but not the dog walker.") then you're in over your head financially. Tip: Lose the dog walker and any other luxury item on your "to pay" list. In tough times stick to the staples: home, heat, gro-ceries, and electricity. You might not think about it, but 20 years ago, nobody had an Internet bill or a cell phone bill. But you probably do now.

If the first step in getting out of financial trouble is knowing that you're in financial trouble, then the next step is to take action to get out of that trouble. First item on the menu is to budget your expenses. I've talked about that extensively in this book. Create a spending plan that allows you to reduce your debts. Itemize your necessary expenses (such as housing and health care) and optional expenses (such as entertainment and vacation travel). Again, make sure you stick to the plan.

Then try to cut out any unnecessary spending such as dining out too much and haunting Circuit City, E-Bay, or Home Depot. Don't be above clipping coupons or purchasing generic products at the supermarket. If you feel you can't resist using your credit card, switch to a bank debit card where money is immediately drawn from your checking account to pay for a purchase.

If you have revolving credit card debt, try using money from your savings account (normally savings accounts are low-paying interest accounts) and use the cash to pay off your high-interest-rate credit card bill.

Above all else, formulate a financial plan for the short and long term that includes a monthly budget and a savings account deposit goal of six months of your annual salary. Build a plan that will allow you to meet your basic life needs and one that will allow you to sleep at night. If you do create and maintain such a plan, you'll be sleeping like a baby before you know it—and not a red flag in sight.

WHAT IS DEBT MANAGEMENT?

Managing your student loan debt is just a piece of your overall debt puzzle. And recognizing red flags that indicate you are in trouble is another.

The bigger picture—how debt can impact your life, the steps you can take to control debt, credit and borrowing issues, and who to go to for help if you need professional debt counseling—is the underpinning of the debt management structure.

It's also important to understand what debt management is not. It's not, for example, another name for bankruptcy, although that's a common misnomer. Debt management doesn't mean you are in bankruptcy, or even on the way there. Bankruptcy is usually reserved for those who can't pay their debts and need legal protection. Debt management is reserved for those who can pay their debts, but need a little help in doing so.

Put it this way:

- Bankruptcy is permanent and debt management is temporary.
- Bankruptcy is for people who don't even have enough cash on hand to pay for food and shelter. Debt management is for people who can't afford to pay all of their debt obligations.
- Bankruptcy is for people who have no money to pay creditors. Debt management is for people who have simply fallen behind on their payments to creditors.
- Bankruptcy is for people who can only afford to pay cents on the dollar on their debts. Debt management is for people who plan on paying 100 percent of their debts (with a potential break on interest, depending on the good graces of their creditors).
- Bankruptcy is for people who will soon lose some, most, or all of their assets. Debt management is for people who don't lose assets.
- Bankruptcy is for people who may never get credit again. Debt management is for people who will get credit again.

In short, debt management is a viable alternative to bankruptcy for those individuals who can afford to meet their debt obligations. But note that if a bleak debt situation goes largely ignored, the path from debt management to bankruptcy can be a short one.

DEBT MANAGEMENT JOB ONE
The Importance of Knowing Your Credit Score

How do you start your debt management strategy? By knowing where you stand, debt-wise. This means knowing what credit report bureaus and lending and credit organizations think of you. Not as a person per se, but as a credit risk.

PREAPPROVED CREDIT CARD OFFER? HERE'S HOW TO PROTECT YOURSELF

Who hasn't opened up their mailbox to find a preapproved credit card offer or two? A cynic might say that whole forests have been toppled for the sole reason of getting your signature on a shiny new credit card.

And why not? Americans love abusing their credit cards. The average U.S. household credit debt rose from $2,985 in 1990 to more than $8,100 last year as the number of credit cards in use increased from 250 million to 538.1 million, according to credit card site CardWeb.com.

The best way to keep credit card debt down is to not use a credit card. But if you do receive a preapproved card that intrigues you, at least know what you're getting into before signing on the bottom line:

- **What interest am I paying?** Make sure you understand the interest rate you will be paying and for how long. Usually, fixed-rate annual percentage rates (APRs) are the best deal, because credit card companies have to notify you before raising rates (variable-rate cards rise and fall with prime interest rates).

- **Know that rates can vary.** You may not know it but most credit cards carry more than one interest rate; balance transfers and cash advances usually carry a higher rate. Consequently, you may have a 12.9 percent APR on purchases and a 19.6 percent APR on cash advances. Not surprisingly, credit card companies apply any monthly payments to the part of the balance that is subject to the lowest interest rate, before the higher-rate part is paid.

- **Don't pay late.** Tardy credit card bill payers can expect the back of the credit card industry's hand in the form of higher interest rates. Some cards will immediately raise your interest rate from the introductory teaser rate to the regular rate if you're late just one time.

- **Pay no fees.** If there's a fee involved with your new credit card offer, walk away. Why pay a fee for a credit card when, with good credit, you don't have to?

- **Cyber shopper? Get protection.** If you like to shop on the Internet, get a credit card with a safe online shopping guarantee. Look for a card with specific guarantees, such as 100 percent coverage for any losses resulting from fraud when shopping on the Internet.

- **Don't assume you'll get approved.** Preapproved credit card offers are no guarantee of credit. If you return the card offer, many financial institutions will conduct a "postscreening" process, which typically involves reviewing your credit bureau report in full as well as verifying information provided on your application. If your financial situation has changed, or if the card-issuing institution determines through postscreening that you don't qualify for the credit line initially, you may still be offered a card, but with different terms or a smaller credit line. Or your application may be turned down.

- **How can I get these guys off my back?** If you don't want to receive preapproved card offers, call 888-5OPT-OUT to get your credit file blocked against prescreening at the three major credit bureaus.

One of the best ways to do that is to know your credit score. Credit scores are the answer to the question, "How can debt problems be cut off in advance?" Credit scores are the marks that credit report agencies bestow upon you and share with the rest of the world—or at least with the part of the world that might want to extend a loan to you or green-light good credit for you.

You'd think people would want to know what credit score they've been given and what that score means to their lives. When you think about it, your credit score is a huge factor in your life. It can mean the difference between owning a house or renting one, going to an Ivy League school or a community college, or driving a new Lexus or an old LeBaron.

But people don't seem to care what their credit score is. In fact, it's downright funny how some people can rattle off trivial information at the drop of a hat but have no clue when it comes to knowing their financial status. You want the lowdown on the latest Hollywood scandal? No problem, got it all for you right here. What's that recipe for Bruschetta? Wait, I have it here in my back pocket.

What's my credit score? Ummmhh . . . what's a credit score?

So hear me out. Knowing your credit score and what it can mean to your financial future is a big deal. While knowing the latest Hollywood gossip or having the secret ingredient for that to-die-for party dish may pay off in your social circle, knowing your credit score—and knowing how to improve it—offers significantly greater rewards. Say, a better house or a good college education for your children.

Why the onus on credit scores? And what are they? Credit scores, also known as FICO scores, are used by creditors to figure out if you're a good credit risk or not. It tells them whether it's a good bet that you'll pay off that student loan or make payments on that new big-screen television in a timely fashion.

Creditors make those calculations based on the data included in your credit report. As a U.S. citizen, and presumably the owner of a Social Security number, your financial history is a public record. In virtually all cases, your financial background can be found, condensed and including payment history, at any one of three credit report agencies (I covered them in Chapter 3, but here they are again): Equifax, Experian, and TransUnion. Each of these companies is a veritable clearinghouse of personal financial information of anybody, citizen or not, with a U.S. Social Security number. The information each provides can make or break some of your biggest financial moves, from owning a home to opening your own business.

Credit scoring mechanisms are fairly easy to understand. A credit score in the low 600s signals a problem for a lender. That doesn't mean you can't get a loan, but it likely means you'll pay a higher interest rate to get it. On the other hand, a score in the upper 700s is a joy to behold for a lender—and for you, too, because you'll probably get the loan at a lower rate because you're such a good credit risk.

Credit agencies look at people with similar financial backgrounds and habits to assign your score. That model includes past credit history, any big purchases made (and whether they were paid off or not), and job and income estimates. Based on the collective "credit history" of loads of people who are a mirror image of you financially, your credit score is meant to forecast you future abilities to handle debt and make timely payments to lenders and creditors.

Your credit score is based on five key financial criteria:

1. **Payment history.** About 35 percent of your credit score is based on your bill payment history.
2. **Amounts owed.** About 30 percent of your score is based on the amount of money you currently owe.
3. **Length of credit history.** About 15 percent of your score is based on how long you've been taking on bills—and paying them.
4. **How much credit?** About 10 percent of your score is based on new credit activity.
5. **Types of credit.** About 10 percent of your score is based on the kinds of credit you have, for example, car payments,

mortgage payments, credit card bills, school loans, and the like.

Lenders and creditors also prefer to look at public record and collection items—things such as bankruptcies, judgments, suits, liens, wage attachments, and collection items. These are considered red flags by lenders, although older items will count less than recent ones.

They'll also dig a bit deeper and check out details on late or missed payments and public record and collection items—specifically, how late they were, how much was owed, how recently they occurred, and how many there were. A 30-day late payment is not as risky as a 90-day late payment, for example. But recent bill payment activity and frequency count, too. A 30-day late payment made just a month ago will count more than a 90-day late payment from five years ago. Note that closing an account on which you had previously missed a payment does not make the late payment disappear from your credit report.

What's not part of your credit score? Things such as your income and bank balance, the interest rates you pay on other loans, your occupation, job title, employer, time with your company, and employment history do not count on your credit score.

What Can Hurt Your Score

Credit scores are dynamic, meaning they change all the time. A bank lender checking your credit rating may come up with a completely different score than an auto loan company that checks your report 15 minutes later. That's because bill payment information is coming into the credit-rating agencies all the time, impacting your score one way or another. Here are a few ways to lower your score:

Repeated inquiries. Each time you apply for credit and a credit grantor requests your credit report, a few points may be deducted on the theory that you are adding to your potential monthly obligations.

Preapproved credit cards. If you have a history of accepting preapproved credit cards, your credit score may be lowered on the theory that too many cards equals too much debt. A person with one credit card is going to score much higher than a person with six credit cards because, in theory, the former has much less debt than the latter.

Late or no payments. Any college graduate can tell you that being late just one payment on a college loan—or worse, not paying the bill at all—can cost you your first home. Lenders take bill payment seriously. If you're habitually late paying one bill, they take the position that you'll be late paying their loan, too.

How to Improve Your Score

In general, late payments will lower your score, but a good record of making payments on time will raise your score. So the obvious place to start improving your credit score (after obtaining a copy of your credit report from Equifax, Experian, or Trans-Union) is to ensure that all your bills are paid on time.

Besides paying your bills on time, don't let your credit card and revolving balances get too high. Even if you pay the bare minimum on your Visa card, a potential lender may see your high level of revolving card debt and assume you can't keep up with your financial obligations.

Also check your credit reports for errors. The fact that you ultimately paid off your college loan may be lost in a sea of bureaucratic paperwork that the credit-rating agency never sees. So check and see that all the data on your credit report is accurate.

One quick way to do that is to check the three major credit report companies: Equifax (http://www.equifax.com), Experian (http://www.experian.com), and TransUnion Credit Bureau (http://www.transunion.com). Each provides your credit-rating report and handles stolen card and fraud complaints.

Once you get your credit report, be sure all the accounts listed on the report are actually your own and dispute negative information if it is wrong. And if positive information is missing, insist that your creditors report it.

Above all, take nothing for granted. Your financial future may be riding on your credit score.

CORRECTING CREDIT REPORT MISTAKES

H. L. Mencken once said that for every problem, there is a solution that is simple, neat, and wrong. Some might say that's a good description of the credit report industry, where mistakes, unfortunately, are as common as flies at a July 4th picnic. When errors are made on your credit, you and you alone suffer the consequences.

That's why knowing your credit value and knowing what information is included on your credit report are two big first steps in smart debt management. Why? Because if you are aware of this information, you can eliminate any nasty surprises that might be in store for you. For example, you're down at Gimbels or Marshall Field's and you can't wait to open up your new charge card. But when the clerk comes back, with what you swear is a smirk on her face, you know right away that you're application for credit has been rejected. Nine times out of ten that means you weren't aware of your credit score or weren't aware of what was on your credit report. In other words, you didn't have control over your debt management situation (of course, opening a department store charge card is another example of that).

Okay, so what happens if that situation *does* come to pass and you get rejected for credit? And you swear that you've paid your bills and you swear that your credit is clean? Could be that there is a mistake on your credit report—and you need to fix it. If you don't, the error stays on your credit report for seven years, for all to see. You don't want that to happen.

Unfortunately, many Americans do. According to *Consumer Reports* magazine, 48 percent of Americans have mistakes on their credit reports, with 12 percent of those mistakes severe enough to restrict those consumers from getting credit. Consequently, it's always best to check your credit report before you apply for a big loan or buy something on credit. That way you can correct any mistakes you find on your report before a lender or creditor notices.

In most cases, credit errors are caused by that most banal of reasons—your name. The more common it is, the higher the chance that you may share someone else's financial faux pas—someone with the same name as you. Maybe that person dies, maybe that person stopped paying off his or her student loans, or maybe that person's name wound up on your credit report through a transcription error. Most often, the name situation will come to manifest itself on your credit report as an account that doesn't belong to you.

To fix credit errors like that, make sure to check out all three credit report agencies. Do so at least once annually. One report agency may have different information than another so you have to cover all your bases.

When you identify an error, get cracking. By law, credit agencies are required to fix any errors. But don't hold your breath, because they don't always move as fast as you'd like. Or as fast as you need if you have a big mortgage loan waiting.

To get things going, file a dispute with the agency. You can call or e-mail, or even place a phone call (if you go that route make sure you jot down the name and title of the person you speak to).

Any written correspondence should include the following information:

- Your name, address, date of birth, and Social Security number
- The name of the company you have a dispute with and any relevant account numbers
- The reason for your dispute, any corrections to your personal information, and a request for correction

Make sure that you collect all the paperwork you need to document your side of the story before you contact the credit agency. Assume nothing and be prepared for anything and any question. Make no mistake, the credit bureau will want solid proof that they have made a mistake.

L *o* *a* *n* **S** *n* *a* *p* *s* *h* *o* *t*

GET YOUR SIDE OF THE STORY OUT THERE

If you can't get a credit bureau to correct a mistake, you can get them to at least print your side of the story on a given dispute and include it on your credit report.

SHOULD YOU HANDLE YOUR OWN DEBT MANAGEMENT ISSUES?

Identifying and attempting to correct debt problems is critical to solving those problems. For some individuals, identifying debt problems is as far as they want to go. After that, it's time to pass off the baton to a professional debt counselor or credit repair company. In some cases, a financial advisor or attorney might even be brought into the picture. For others, handling debt problems, with all the correspondence, phone calls, debt negotiations, and other issues that come part and parcel with debt management problems, is easy.

As usual, there are pros and cons to the issue. If you are a hands-on type and understand financial issues, it's entirely plausible and understandable that you could tackle your debt challenges yourself. But if the thought of negotiating with creditors, writing strong letters to credit bureaus, and all those other tough tasks you have to tackle as your own debt manager sends you swooning, then hiring a reputable debt management professional is a good way to go. I'll get to the question of hiring a professional shortly. Let's address the do-it-yourself question first.

Being Your Own Debt Manager

The primary advantage of being your own debt management advisor is that nobody knows your personal financial situation like you do. There's no explaining to a third-party advisor what debts you owe, how much money you've borrowed, or any medical issues or job loss issues that contributed to your debt problems.

That information comes in handy when you begin doing your own debt negotiations with creditors and lenders. It's a do-it-yourself approach that doesn't come without risk, but if you know what you're doing, you can save your own bacon if debt gets too heavy for you.

Debt negotiation, also known as debt arbitration or debt settlement, is a sensitive, yet critical, issue. Basically, debt negotiation is a last resort before you start looking at bankruptcy (an issue with which you definitely need professional help). Of course, in some instances, like when an old, forgotten debt suddenly pops up on a credit report (e.g., an old utility bill from college that you paid but your roommates didn't), debt negotiation is much easier and can be resolved with a short payment plan with, for example, no interest payments.

The idea behind do-it-yourself debt negotiations is to reduce or minimize the payments you make to a creditor with whom you are, most likely, already in arrears. You can begin doing that by contacting the creditor directly and seeing if they're amenable to you skipping a payment, knocking a few bucks off your payment, or, as I mentioned previously, eliminating any interest payments. Can't hurt to ask, right?

Another solution is to consolidate your debts, an issue I cover extensively in Chapter 6. Consolidating buys you some time and bundles all your loans and debts into one payment.

If you do handle your own debt negotiations, be prepared to:

- **Pay some money up front.** Most lenders may want at least 50 percent of your overall loan up front (although that figure, too, is negotiable). Note that some creditors won't even begin to negotiate until they receive *some* money from you.
- **Deal with an attorney.** Most creditors have agents or customer service reps handle some debt negotiations. But at some point be prepared to see a lawyer get involved who is representing the creditor. Usually, there has to be a substantial amount of debt before this happens.
- **Send a money order for any credit payments.** If you make any payments with your personal checks your creditor has obtained, in the process, all your pertinent banking information. What's the problem? If you're sued, it's simple for the creditor to get at your funds through your bank account.
- **Prioritize how any settlement will look on your all-important credit report statement.** "Fully paid" or "Debt satisfied" is the language you're looking for. "Debt still active" is not what you're looking for.
- **Bring a lawyer in to shore up your defense.** If negotiations go nowhere, or if either party does not live up to their end of the bargain, the lawsuits can start to fly.
- **Be realistic.** You might back down a bit and okay a repayment deal that is still too much for you. Don't agree to any debt payment plan that you can't pay.
- **Find out how far the creditor is willing to go.** If a creditor offers three months at no interest, ask for six. Always aim high. And know how much negotiating room you have to work with.
- **Pay less for a lump-sum payment but demand that the debt be shown as "Paid in full" on your credit report.** Creditors will usually settle for less on the dollar so they get something back. Once they get that, your creditor may be willing to strike any mention of debt from your credit report. Again, it doesn't hurt to ask.

GETTING PROFESSIONAL HELP

Taking debt management matters into your own hands is commendable. After all, if you have tried something and failed, you are still vastly better off than if you tried nothing and succeeded. Still, taking the solo route may not be viable for many people. Lack of time, lack of education, or simply lack of interest may spur some folks on to going out and getting professional help.

But is a professional debt counselor or credit repair specialist right for you? That's a good question to ask if you have exhausted all your student loan payment options—or other debts—and still feel like you're not getting anywhere.

Of course, there are pros and cons to getting good debt counseling help, too. Yes, having a reputable, smart professional who understands debt on your side can be a big plus in your debt management campaign. On the other hand, there are plenty of fly-by-night, fraudulent debt counselors out there, lurking on the fringes of the financial services industry. Many of them thrive on the Internet, preying on desperate and vulnerable individuals who don't realize that they're placing themselves in deeper financial peril by doing business with debt management con artists.

And even the ethical credit counseling companies will go only so far with you. There's an old story about the tax attorney who told his client on the way to the IRS office, "I did say that as your tax attorney I would accompany you to the IRS in the event of an audit. But I never said that I'd go inside." Similarly, if you ever go to court, you probably won't have your trusty credit service advisor alongside of you. Everyone has their limits.

Chances are, the debt management help you'll be seeking will come from a credit counseling or credit repair service. These are agencies designed especially to help people get out of their debt problems and get on with their lives.

Usually that help comes within the framework of debt management advice or direct intervention on your behalf with your creditors. The idea is to help people manage their debts responsibly and eliminate any debt in the most economically feasible way possible (to you, that is). Credit counselors stand by your side and give you an educated voice. They can play the equalizer role you'll need, given the fact that the creditor will be well armed, too.

You have to be cautious about the type of credit management service you choose. While many are virtuous and ethical, some are not. They may overcharge and underdeliver or offer bad advice. Check with your local consumer protection agency before you hire a credit manager.

L o a n   S n a p s h o t

TIPS ON CHOOSING A CREDIT COUNSELOR

How can you tell if a credit counseling service is reputable? Follow these guidelines:

- Look for credit counselors who don't charge for free information, such as information on legal rights accorded debt sufferers or data on government-sponsored credit programs.
- Make sure you receive a list of what the credit service will do for you before paying them any money. Then only pay if they do what they promised.
- Check with your local consumer protection agency.

Once you begin working with a credit manager, gather all your relevant debt documents, invoices, account statements, and such, make copies, and bring them to the first meeting with your counselor. On the agenda will be scenarios when you begin some type of repayment plan. So be prepared to figure out how much you can afford to pay.

Also note any aggressive collection agencies and ask your credit counselor to help stop them from contacting you. If you have a credit service on your side, they can begin fielding such calls, not you.

That's what you're paying them for in the first place.

MY TAKE

All things being equal, if you create a good, solid debt management framework, one that includes knowing your credit score, knowing what's on your credit report, and knowing how to deal with creditors, lenders, and collection agencies, you really don't need professional help.

Student Loan Case Study

BY THE MANUAL

Kate Chapman, a 27-year-old architect, had made some progress getting out of debt, then slid backward after a six-month layoff.

"I wasn't paying off all my loans and I wanted to negotiate some sort of repayment process with my creditors," she says. "I also wanted to mend any negative data on my credit report."

At work, an associate mentioned how she had used a credit report manual to help her climb out of debt. "She said that the credit repair manual gave her all the information she needed to come up with a debt management program," Chapman adds.

Chapman went on the Internet and found a credit repair manual and purchased it. "I saw some free e-books and white papers on the topic of credit repair and they were useful, too," she says, "but I wanted a book I could carry around with me and browse while I had lunch."

Using the information in the book, which included sections on debt negotiation and dealing with credit and collection agencies, Chapman soon had a do-it-yourself debt strategy she could count on.

"You've got to use the information you find in a credit repair manual," she says. "If you do, you're already halfway there."

The key is finding your comfort level. If you can't sleep at night worrying about your student loan debt, and have exhausted all other options, maybe having a professional on your side is right for you. But short of that, try to handle debt issues on your own before paying someone else to do it.

As I said before, nobody is as interested—or has as much at stake—in your financial affairs as you do. In that regard, you are your own best debt management advocate.

CHAPTER REVIEW

- Be aware of your financial red flags.
- Know your credit score.
- Be able to deal with creditors.
- Use a professional credit counseling service if you must. But choose wisely.

8

OTHER SMART FINANCIAL MOVES FOR STUDENT LOAN BORROWERS

Imet a friend recently who runs his own business, a graphic design business. He told me that business was terrific. In fact, he said things were so swell that he had enough money to last him the rest of his life—as long as he dies by next Wednesday.

That's the problem with managing debt. It's good to pay it off but if you don't take other steps to improve your financial situation, then you're holding yourself back from meeting those long-term financial goals you want to attain. You know, things like owning a home, marrying and starting a family, running your own business, retiring early with lots of money in the bank—things like that.

That's why making room for a long-range investment campaign alongside your student loan repayment campaign is such a good idea, if a little intimidating.

Having worked on Wall Street, I know that you can grow wealth while eliminating debt at the same time. In fact, it's easier than you think. I repeat: There is no reason why you can't pay your student loan debt while simultaneously laying the groundwork for your financial future through saving and investing.

Obviously, as I've been harping on for the past seven chapters, paying off your student loan debt is a big part of setting the table for your financial future, but it's not the only item on the menu. You can pay off your debt quickly and cleanly, and simultaneously begin erecting the building blocks that will help secure your financial future.

Some of those measures I'll be talking about—setting your financial goals, investing in your company retirement plan, and using index-based mutual funds—are pretty big items. Admittedly, I can't cover in one chapter how important these items are in your financial planning arsenal. But I can introduce you to the concepts of these sound financial planning tools and explain how they can help you build a financial nest egg even as you are paying off your student loan debt.

That scenario is not only possible but highly advisable. Let's take a look.

SETTING YOUR LONG-TERM FINANCIAL GOALS

So far, I've spent the bulk of this book talking about debt issues and how to resolve them. I'm not really finished talking about debt; I'll have more resources and tips on the subject in Chapters 9 and 10, but I wanted to take some time to talk about the other half of the financial planning equation—saving money.

Think of managing debt and managing investments in the following context. By tackling debt issues, including building a budget, understanding credit card debt, establishing a good record-keeping system, and paying off your debt, you're establishing the foundation for your financial future. With an investment strategy, you're pouring the concrete.

The first step in the investment process is establishing long-term financial goals. Whether it's a 1-year plan to pay for your wedding, a 10-year plan to begin investing in your child's college education, or a 30-year plan to save for retirement, establishing finite financial goals down the road a piece is a winning situation.

Achieve most of your goals—or come close—and you have measurable proof that you are headed in the right direction. Fall short, and it's a headslap that more drastic steps may be necessary.

Unfortunately, we're seeing more of the latter these days. A recent survey by a Big Six accounting firm shows that unless we save a great deal more than we currently do, three out of four Americans over the age of 20 will have less than half the money they need to retire and maintain their preretirement standard of living. In fact, on average they would have to reduce their expenses by 60 percent or get a job flipping burgers—to make it through their twilight years without running out of money.

Let's put it in more exact terms. If your after-tax expenses currently run $50,000 a year and you retire today, you would have to cut your spending by at least $30,000 if you want your money to last as long as you do. And that huge cut in your budget assumes that you have the good sense to die on the day you spend your last penny. If you survive longer than the actuaries estimate, you'll outlive your money. Yes, as a recent college graduate you aren't likely to retire soon, but you'd be surprised how fast the time goes. The last thing you want after paying off your student loan debts is to be behind the curve on building a financial nest egg. As you'll see later on in this chapter, investing early and investing often is *by far* the best ways to get rich.

That's why setting long-term financial goals is so critical. Fortunately, it's also pretty easy. Here are some ideas for younger investors (investors in their 20s and 30s) that will help you establish your financial planning game plan:

- **Be specific.** Aim for clear targets such as "$2,000 into a retirement account," rather than generalities like "contribute to savings." Your company's 401(k) plan can help here (more on that shortly).
- **Put pay raises directly into savings or toward debt reduction.** Got a raise? Great. But there's no rule that says you

have to spend it. After all, if you make ends meet now, then you don't need to live off the cash you get in a pay raise. Put the extra money from a raise or a bonus where it will do the most good, either increasing retirement savings or trimming your student loan debt. I'd use it to pay off your student loan debt first and then apply anything left to your financial investment portfolio. In this way, you maximize the good of the pay raise and move toward long-term goals without reducing your standard of living.

- **Invest in stocks.** It is virtually impossible to beat inflation and generate a decent return without investing in the stock market. You're taking on investment risk, but you are avoiding inflation risk, and if you have a diversified portfolio, you are spreading your investment risk. Inflation risk isn't to be understated, even though it's been relatively nonexistent for the past several years. Let's say you're heavily invested in Treasury bonds that pay 6 percent interest. Inflation suddenly spikes upward to 10 percent. You're now losing money and the only way to compensate is to sell those investments at a loss and reinvest the money or to continue falling further behind in real income because inflation is outstripping the return on your investments.

- **Estimate how much you'll need to retire in comfort.** I know, it's hard to figure out what you'll need in retirement when you just got out of school. But bear with me. You may not want to stay in your current job forever; you might want to start your own business someday or try to retire early. These, too, are long-term goals that need to be factored into your financial plan. Start with a rough estimate based on what you earn now. If you expect to lead a more modest life in retirement, use 60 percent to 70 percent of your current income. If the future holds too many unknowns, however, start with 100 percent. Then tackle more detailed financial calculations, either on your own or with the help of financial planners, to assess such factors as the likely impact inflation will have on your purchasing power.

- **Develop a savings plan.** How far away you are from retirement plays a large part in how you should invest your retirement money. Historically, there are three stages to a long-term regular savings plan for retirement: capitalization, consolidation, and conservation. In the first stage, the one you're likely in, people should be most concerned with building up their retirement savings portfolio. These investors can take as aggressive an outlook as their nerves can stand because at this point there is little capital to risk. The second step, consolidation, makes up the bulk of your savings plan; here is when you balance the aggressive investments with some tamer ones, to better protect your existing assets. The final change, from consolidation to conservation, when your investments should aim to preserve the capital you have, should take place one to three years before you retire. The exact timing of all these should take current market conditions into account.
- **Start saving now.** You'll need to save enough from your 30-odd years of working to live for about 30 years in retirement. So get cracking. When you do ramp up your savings program, overestimate your needs. It's far better to end up with too much money than not enough. Even a little bit more a year can make a difference in the long term.
- **Get some good life insurance.** Solid life insurance is critical to your fiscal fitness, even if you're young and single. If you're out of commission, or worse, chances are you may not have enough life insurance to protect you or your loved ones. Usually, several hundred thousand dollars of term life is the way to go. Term insurance is generally the most inexpensive way to insure a life.

THE ADVANTAGES OF INVESTING EARLY

One of Aesop's classic fables concerns the squirrel that started stocking up early for the long, cold winter ahead and the frivolous squirrel that didn't. When winter came, the second squirrel could

L *o a n*   **S** *n a p s h o t*

THE RULE OF 72

Here's a trick some financial planners use. To find out how many years it will take your investment to double, divide the annual rate of return by 72. So at a 7 percent return from your 401(k) plan last year, your money will double in 10 years and quadruple in 20 years. Financial gurus call it "the rule of 72."

only gaze enviously at the pile of acorns the first squirrel had safely tucked away up in his tree. Moral of the story: Start piling up your acorns early. In other words, the sooner you start to plan for your financial future, the faster you're going to obtain wealth.

But some people can't be bothered. Even in the context of this book, people might say, "Gee, I'd love to start saving, but I have all these student loans to pay off and a life to live, so . . . sorry. Maybe next year." But as I've been saying, it is possible to pay off your loans and invest for your future. And despite what you might hear from the newspapers, investing is a young person's game, because you have time on your side, you can take more investment risk, and, consequently, you can accumulate more money.

Some people don't get that and wind up procrastinating. But saving for your financial future should have started long before you turn 40. If you don't start saving until your 40s, you'll need to set aside 20 percent of your gross income for your retirement or for that new business you want to open up. If you wait until your 50s, your target will have to be 30 percent. As a last resort, you may have to sell your house, your cottage, and your second car; get a second job; and reduce your leisure spending.

But if you're in your 20s or 30s, you can take more risk and accumulate more money. That doesn't mean putting all your money in penny stocks. But it does mean placing a greater percentage of your investments in higher-earning equities rather than the more cautious Treasury and savings bonds that many people select as they get older.

Consider these examples:

- If you start investing $100 a month at age 25 in a retirement account that gains 10 percent a year, by age 65 you'll have $632,000. But if you don't start investing the same amount until you're 35, you'll take away only $226,000 when you retire. Starting at 25 will get you $406,000 more, at a cost of only $12,000.
- If you set aside $200 a month at a 10.2 percent return, you could start investing at age 21 and stop 10 years later and have a $1 million nest egg at age 65. That means a $22,000 investment over a single decade gets you $1 million down the road. Of course, assuming continued inflation, $1 million then won't buy you what $1 million would today. But it'll buy you a heck of a lot more than nothing will.

BUILDING BLOCKS

Once you've determined that you want to begin your investment plan, even while you're paying off your student loans, it's time to sit down and go to work building your investment portfolio. When you start looking for the right portfolio, keep things simple at first.

In fact, most investment portfolios are comprised of five or so components. Usually, they include some combination of the following:

1. Liquid assets (cash and equivalents)
2. Fixed income (bonds and annuities)
3. Equities (stocks)
4. Real estate
5. Precious metals and other investments

PREPARED FOR THE WORST?

Saving through investing isn't just a great idea for your long-term financial future, it can help out when things go wrong, too. Ask yourself these questions before you decide not to pursue a savings plan:

- If you're hit with an unexpected large expense—the refrigerator died, your car brakes failed, a rotted tree in your yard has to go—how would you pay for it?
- If your spouse died tomorrow, would you know how much money is available for you to carry on, including life insurance, investments, and savings? Would you know to whom you owe money?
- If you were sued for $1 million, what would you do?
- If you lost your job this week, do you have a backup plan? What if you were injured and were told you couldn't work for six months?
- If your parent suffered a debilitating stroke or other life-threatening illness, what action would you take? How would medical or nursing-home expenses affect your own finances?
- If your children (or future children) want to attend an out-of-state private college, how would you pay for it?
- Finally, for your own financial peace of mind, how much money would you need to accumulate for you to say, "I have enough"?

Most investment programs will include only stocks and bonds, although some include money market instruments or real estate investment trusts. In this chapter, I'm concentrating only on stocks and bonds, the cornerstones of any investment portfolio.

For the purposes of this book, and its postcollege graduate audience, let me explain how to build a good investment plan through a vehicle that we all know and love—the 401(k) plan. After that, I'll talk about some of the elements that go into a good, long-term investing plan, whether your use a 401(k) plan or not.

L o a n   S n a p s h o t

TAKE STOCK

According to financial industry calculations, stocks have returned, on average, 12 percent annually since the experts started tracking such things in 1926.

A 401(k) SURVIVAL GUIDE

Investing in a 401(k) plan or another company-sponsored retirement plan such as an Individual Retirement Account is a no-brainer for workers just out of college. As I'll explain, you'll barely miss the money that's taken out of your paycheck when you invest in such a plan and that means you can still easily pay off your student loan at the same time. Plus, by investing in a long-term retirement plan early, you're chances of being a millionaire in your 50s is actually pretty good, as long as you contribute to your plan early and often.

Lately, however, 401(k) plans have gotten an unfair rap, in my opinion. In the dot.com days of yore, when Internet millionaires walked the earth, the idea of waiting 30 or 40 years to cash in on the easy life was held in low regard by many American workers. What self-respecting software engineer or manufacturing line supervisor would give up on the notion of instant riches through the stock market and its erstwhile cousin, the stock option? The 401(k) plan, only 20 years old or so at the time, was viewed by many employees as quaint—a sideshow to the Greatest Show on Earth currently playing at your local dot.com company or venture capital start-up.

True, many 401(k) portfolios suffered significant losses when stocks fell dramatically in the early 2000s. And true, the corporate scandals of the same era gave 401(k)s a black eye, fairly or unfairly. But compared to the worthless pieces of paper that most stock option holders held during the 1990s, 401(k) plans still look very good in the 2000s, especially as the markets have begun to return to the days of double-digit annual investment returns. Their built-in diversity and interest-compounding features have helped 401(k) plans survive the economic perils that pretty much finished off the employee stock option, the day traders, and other dot.com investment portfolio wildlife.

L *o a n* **S** *n a p s h o t*

NO 401(k)/STUDENT LOAN ARRANGEMENT

Keep your company retirement plan and your student loan separate. Taking money out of your 401(k) or IRA early results in IRS penalties. Plus, it's money and interest you'll never earn back. Keep the two separate.

SOME 401(k) ADVICE YOU CAN TAKE TO HEART (AND THEN TO THE BANK)

Investing in your 401(k) like a Wall Street professional isn't difficult. Just follow the following six steps and you'll be on your way:

1. **Start early.** As I've said, there's no substitute for getting a good start on your financial future. All the studies on the subject conclude that the earlier you get going with your 401(k), the more money you'll have in retirement. That's because the earlier you start, the earlier compound interest goes to work for you. Start in your 20s if you can. If you start later, make sure to max out your contributions to catch up. Some good news from Uncle Sam: The new tax law provides a "catch-up" statute that allows workers over 50 to add more into their 401(k)s on an annual basis to make up for late starts.

2. Go the limit. A 401(k) provides a multitude of benefits for the investor. One of the most beneficial is the plan's tax-advantaged status. In short, the more you contribute to your 401(k) plan every year, the less you'll pay in taxes to Uncle Sam (plus, the new tax law raises the annual contribution limits to $15,000 by 2006). Most companies will offer a company match as well. That means for every dollar you toss into your 401(k) plan up to a certain percent (usually between 3 percent and 6 percent of your annual contributions), your company may match it. Note: Your company may elect to match your contribution in company stock instead of cash. A little company stock is okay, but as Enron demonstrated, too much company stock can spell disaster. When it comes to company matching, cash is king.

3. Do your homework. The value of good investment research is priceless. And the value of knowing enough about your 401(k) to become the master of your financial future is priceless. Read all you can on finance and investments, and make sure you read every seemingly boring word of the 401(k) packets, brochures, and memoranda that come your way from your employer each year. Yes, I know that this stuff can read like *The Tibetan Book of the Dead,* but it's time well spent when you're planning to get wealthy. When it comes to making investment choices, assess your own risk level. Will you sleep at night with a portfolio jammed with company stock? Such a portfolio worked great for Microsoft employees in recent years, but certainly not for Enron employees. The rule of thumb is to have no more than 20 percent of company stock in your 401(k).

4. Be aggressive. Prudence is the proper course if you're an airplane pilot or a brain surgeon. But it's a drawback for 401(k) investors. Studies show that to beat inflation and to make your money grow faster, a good chunk of your plan should be earmarked for higher-performing stock funds. That doesn't mean you should be reckless. There's no rule that says you have to put money into Portuguese debentures because your buddy in accounting did.

But leaning toward stocks, especially in your 20s, 30s and 40s, is the way to build a hefty 401(k) plan for the long haul. As I've been saying, the younger you are, the more risk you can take with stock mutual funds. But as you get older, mixing in some more conservative bond funds is a good idea.

5. Keep your eyes on the prize. When you get your quarterly statement, give it a good look, primarily to see how your plan is faring and what kind of fees you're paying. But don't panic if your 401(k) suffers a bad quarter or two. That happens on Wall Street. If after a year your 401(k) is still in decline, however, consider replacing poor performing funds with others that fit your investment profile. A financial advisor is a great idea here. Getting an advisor might cost you several hundred dollars, but an advisor can get a poor-performing 401(k) back on the right track and save you thousands, if not more, in the process.

6. Don't take money out. Some employees who leave their jobs are given the option of taking the cash and rolling it over into another tax-deferred investment plan like a 401(k) or IRA or taking the money in a lump sum and using it as they wished. The latter is a bad move and here's why: the government wants you to roll over the money and it has set up expensive traps if you don't. The IRS can take up to 20 percent of your retirement plan assets away from you if you elect to take a lump-sum payout when you leave a job. If that's not grim news, consider this: it'll also tax you on the capital gains your money has earned while participating in the plan. (When you sell an investment for more than you paid, your profit is called a capital gain. It can be taxed at a rate as high as 28 percent of your earnings.)

COMMONLY ASKED QUESTIONS
ABOUT YOUR 401(k)

Not many people know it, but 401(k) plans haven't been around that long—since 1980 when Congress gave the go-ahead to companies to create their own defined contribution plans. Before then, most companies offered pension plans, where the responsibility for choosing investments and tracking portfolio performance fell on employers and not employees. But then the 401(k) plan came along, where the opposite occurred. Now employees call their own shots, pick their own mutual funds, and decide how much they will invest in them.

This doesn't mean you have to go it alone when handling your 401(k) plan. Virtually every company offering them is eager to help employees with their plans. Most also offer access to the investment companies that distribute and manage 401(k) plans for companies.

One place to start with questions on your 401(k) plan is your company's human resources area. HR staffers are trained to keep up with the latest in 401(k) plan developments and to keep you informed about your company's plan and procedures.

What questions can you ask your HR department? Here's a sampling:

What benefits do I get from a 401(k) plan? The primary benefit is that you're not taxed currently on the portion of compensation that is placed in the plan. You also have the option of choosing between cash or future benefits on a year-to-year basis, thus protecting you in the event of a short-term financial emergency.

Another benefit of a 401(k) plan is that the contributions you make to the plan accumulate tax-free until you retire and begin withdrawing funds from the plan. But in retirement, you'll likely be in a much lower tax bracket than in your earning years.

The 401(k) plan also offers an employee a matching provision in which the employer makes a contribution to the plan equal to (a certain percentage of) your contribution. Basically, it's free money—and the more you invest, the more your company will match (up to a limit).

How much can I contribute every year? While I was writing this book in 2003, Uncle Sam allowed 401(k) plan participants to contribute $15,000 to their 401(k)s (up from $10,000 in 1999).

What does pretax mean? When you contribute to your 401(k) account, money gets invested before federal and most state income taxes are calculated. This means you are being taxed on less money than you've actually earned. Your money goes to work for you and continues to grow, earning interest and capital gains on a tax-deferred basis.

How do I make contributions to the plan? It's easy. Your company simply withholds your 401(k) contribution from your paycheck and redirects it to the investment firm managing your 401(k). Because your contribution is tax-free, you'll hardly notice the reduction in your pay.

Where does my plan money go? An estimated 45 percent of 401(k) plan assets were held in mutual funds at year-end 2000. The remainder of assets were managed by insurance companies, banks, and other institutions.

Also, don't be reluctant to ask about 401(k) plan fees. Most don't charge commissions and it's a big red flag if they do. The investment firm that manages your plan is paid a fee based on the percentage of your 401(k) plans assets. But some companies handle fees differently. So make sure to ask your HR rep how plan and fee expenses are paid and what your portion of the bill is.

While you may not get answers to your 401(k) questions right away, you'll get them eventually. It's in a company's best interests if its employees know what they're doing when it comes to managing their 401(k)s.

INVESTMENT PREPARATION RESOURCES

Here are some good investment resources for younger investors.

The Wealthy Barber, updated Third Edition
By David Chilton; Prima Publishing

A Random Walk Down Wall Street (Fifth Edition)
by Burton G. Malkiel; W. W. Norton & Company

Capital Ideas
by P. Bernstein; Simon and Schuster

Portfolio Selection (Second Edition)
by Harry M. Markowitz; Blackwell

Fundamentals of Investments (Second Edition)
by Alexander, Sharpe, and Bailey; Prentice Hall

INVESTING IN INDEX MUTUAL FUNDS

Mutual funds have taken a beating in the financial press lately, primarily because a few bad apples engaged in unscrupulous trading practices and got their hands caught in the cookie jar. Shame on those who did so and here's hoping they all do the frog-walk on CNN, overcoats over their head on their way to jail.

But mutual funds remain stable, viable investment vehicles. More than $7 trillion remain invested in funds, making them the most popular investment choice in the world.

To accomplish the goals of this book—to find easily understood and easily accessible investment tools for people who recently graduated from college and are paying off their student loans and getting their financial acts together—index-based mutual funds are a great way to go. They're easy, cheap, and plentiful.

Index funds are the polar opposite of traditional actively-managed mutual funds. Think the Road Runner versus Wiley Coyote. The *Concorde* versus the *Spirit of St. Louis*. NASCAR versus the electric car. That's what actively managed funds are to index funds.

In this case, however, slower is better—and cheaper to invest in, too. Index mutual funds basically guarantee that the fund's performance will match an index. For example, if you invest in a mutual fund that tracks a big index such as the Standard & Poor's 500 or the Dow Jones Industrial Average, your fund will likely match the performance of those indexes over the course of a calendar year.

An index fund provides broad diversification by featuring hundreds of stocks drawn from different industries or sectors, thus helping to limit the negative impact of a downturn in any single stock or sector. Usually they offer better performance. Why? Because according to Standard & Poor's, on average, only 10 percent to 20 percent of mutual fund managers outperform the overall market, so an index fund that's able to approximately match the performance of the overall market will beat 80 percent to 90 percent of all mutual fund managers.

Investors, especially beginners, are attracted to index funds because the returns are relatively dependable, relying solely on the index performance and not on the decisions of a portfolio manager. Investors also like index funds because they're easy to use. Because the index funds are attempting to mirror the indexes they cover, decisions are automatic and transactions are kept to a minimum. A bonus: Because decisions are easy to make, fund companies don't spend a lot of money on high-priced managers to choose stocks. Consequently, expenses tend to be lower than those of actively managed funds. Most stock funds that are actively managed by professionals charge annual fees of 1 percent or more, with some charging more than 2 percent per year, mostly to cover the costs of commissions and research. Actively managed funds often trade the stocks in their portfolios on a frequent basis, which also causes high tax consequences in the form of capital gains paid on securities the fund manager sold at a profit. Those plodding old index funds don't trade often at all, resulting in a much lower tax bill.

INDEX FUNDS SAVE ON FEES

On average, you can save hundreds, if not thousands, of dollars annually by investing in index funds instead of in actively managed mutual funds. The money you save can go straight to paying off your student loan.

So, are index funds for you? They are if you're the type of investor who

- is just starting out and wants to keep things easy,
- doesn't want a lot of investment risk,
- likes to keep mutual fund fees and administrative costs low,
- doesn't want investments to be overly complicated, and
- wants to keep fund tax liability low.

But they're not if you're the type of investor who

- prefers the stock-picking prowess a good fund manager can provide,
- wants better-than-average fund returns—and can accept the accompanying risk of actively managed funds, and
- likes the drama and action that index funds invariably don't provide.

MAKE SURE YOUR CHILDREN DON'T HAVE BIG STUDENT LOAN PROBLEMS

There's at least one more smart financial move you can make beyond paying back your student loans and starting an investment plan—making sure your children don't have to go through the same ordeal (or at least not as expensively).

If you have children or are planning to have children (nieces and nephews count, too), you can do them a big favor by planning ahead to pay for their college education. A great way to do this is to use the increasingly popular 529 College Savings Plan.

The 529 plan, named after the section of the Internal Revenue Service code that spawned the plan in 1996, is a high contribution–limit, tax-friendly college investment plan geared specifically to make the burden of funding a college education or two easier to handle.

While the plan is originally from the federal government, it's up to individual states—32 are participating at last count—to design and deploy the plan to their satisfaction. Soon, all 50 states should have 529 plans, the IRS says.

Currently, states are offering two types of 529 plans: conservative (prepaid tuition) and aggressive (mutual fund) plans. Here's a description of each.

Prepaid Tuition Plans

Prepaid plans guarantee that the savings you make toward college will be enough to pay for college years from now. These 529 plans offer investment return rates of 4 percent or 5 percent, more than enough to keep pace with inflation and the resulting rising cost of a college education. By and large, 529 plan recipients can use the plan proceeds to attend schools away from their home states.

College-Savings Plans

Just like a mutual fund, these plans enable savers to contribute to a pool of money (in this case money that's managed by the state or an outside investment advisor). Such plans steer toward stocks when your child is under ten years of age, then shift toward bonds and cash as your child enters high school. Plan recipients can use the plan proceeds at any accredited school, for tuition, room and board, books, and supplies. If your state's plan is inferior or doesn't disclose performance and fees, you can invest in another

THE 529 LIST

State Listings—Section 529 Plans and Names

Alabama	Prepaid Affordable College Tuition Program (PACT)
Alaska	Advanced College Tuition Payment Program
Arizona	Family College Savings Program
Arkansas	You will need to contact your state treasurer through http://www.nast.net.
California	Golden State Scholarshare Trust
Colorado	CollegeInvest Prepaid Tuition Fund and Scholarship Choice
Connecticut	Higher Education Trust
Delaware	College Investment Plan
Florida	Prepaid College Program
Georgia	HOPE Scholarship Program
Hawaii	College Savings Program
Idaho	College Savings Program
Illinois	College Illinois and Bright Start Savings
Indiana	Family College Savings Plan
Iowa	College Savings Iowa
Kansas	Postsecondary Education Savings Program
Kentucky	College Savings Plan
Louisiana	Student Tuition Assistance and Revenue Trust
Maine	NextGen College Investing Plan
Maryland	Prepaid College Trust
Massachusetts	College Savings Programs
Michigan	Education Trust
Minnesota	EdVest
Mississippi	Prepaid Affordable College Tuition Program
Missouri	Saving for Tuition Program
Montana	Family Education Savings Program
Nevada	Prepaid Tuition Program
New Hampshire	Unique College Investing Plan
New Jersey	Better Education Savings Trust
New Mexico	The Education Plan
New York	College Savings Program
North Carolina	College Vision Fund
North Dakota	College Save
Ohio	CollegeAdvantage Savings Plan
Oklahoma	College Savings Plan
Oregon	College Savings Plan
Pennsylvania	Tuition Account Program
Rhode Island	College Bound
South Carolina	Tuition Prepayment Program
South Dakota	None

THE 529 LIST (continued)

State Listings—Section 529 Plans and Names

Tennessee	Baccalaureate Education System Trust Savings Plan
Texas	Tomorrow Fund
Utah	Educational Savings Plan Trust
Vermont	Higher Education Savings Plan
Virginia	College Savings Plan
Washington	State's Guaranteed Education Tuition Program
Washington D.C.	None
West Virginia	Prepaid College Plan
Wisconsin	EdVest
Wyoming	College Achievement Plan

Source: http://www.cpadvantage.com/resources/articles/planning/section-529-plans.asp.

state's plan. It's up to the states to decide who is going to run the plans—in most cases a Wall Street brokerage or mutual firm (so far Fidelity Investments, Vanguard, and Merrill Lynch have signed on to manage 529 plans).

Perhaps the choicest benefit of 529 plans is their tax-deductibility framework. Although contributions aren't tax-deductible, earnings grow tax-free until the money is withdrawn to pay for tuition or college expenses, and then it is only taxed at the student's typical tax rate. Plus, unlike Education IRAs, annual contributions are not limited. Maximum contributions can total as much as $158,750. Even better, 529 college-savings plans don't penalize higher-earning families who might want to seek financial aid.

Who is a good candidate for a 529 plan? Most likely, parents with college-bound children who have cash to invest for college expenses, who want tax advantages, and/or who want to keep control of funds saved for college. Also, good candidates are grandparents, aunts, and uncles who want to help finance higher education expenses for their college-bound relatives and reduce their own estate taxes—without losing all control of funds gifted away.

When you decide that 529 plans are a good fit, take some time to do some comparison shopping (see Figure 8.1). Begin with your own state's 529 to see if it offers any significant state-tax advantages. Be sure to evaluate additional plan features, such as the option of plan proceeds being used for graduate studies, part-time studies, tuition and room and board, or just tuition expenses. Ask what minimum and maximum allowed contributions are in play. Also ask about time limits on using the account and find out what happens if either the contributor or beneficiary passes away. Does the plan use the same definition of "family" as the IRS does? For instance, Wisconsin's 529 plan requires a two-year minimum investment period so contributions can only be made up to the time a child becomes a college sophomore. In the New York plan, the successor owner is determined through the will or state law of intestacy, not the beneficiary listed on the application.

Also, the figure you decide to invest on a regular basis is the figure that your state's plan will hold you to during the length of the plan—that means, for example, $100 a month now and $100 a month until you take control of the assets when your child marches off to campus. If you deviate from that figure, the IRS can slap a 10 percent fine (of your current assets) on you. Also watch out if you wind up divorced, because each state has a different rules regarding the split-up of 529 assets after a marriage ends.

All in all, the pluses outweigh the minuses when it comes to 529 plans. Start one now and cross "saving for college" off your to-do list.

SUMMING UP

The idea is to pay off your student loans as quickly and as efficiently as possible. That's what I've been saying throughout this book and I'm not going to stop now. That said, there's no reason you can't pay your loans and launch a financial planning program at the same time. Using easy-access tools such as company retirement plans and index mutual funds, you can take a huge step toward financial security while you are still relatively young.

Most people can't say that, but wish they could.

FIGURE 8.1 *Comparing College Savings Plan Options*

Savings Period	Out-of-State 529 Plan*		In-State 529 Plan*		UGMA/ UTMA		Taxable Account Owned by Parent	
	18 Years	8 Years	18 Years	8 Years	18 Years	8 Years	18 Years	8 Years
Amount Invested	$ 90,000	40,000	$ 92,250	41,000	$ 90,000	40,000	$ 90,000	40,000
Earnings	127,632	22,851	130,836	23,428	131,070	24,088	125,615	23,446
Tax Cost (before distributions)	—	—	—	—	9,043	1,058	17,354	3,239
Taxes on Distributions	6,232	993	—	—	4,142	523	8,392	1,566
After-tax Earnings for College	211,400	61,858	223,086	64,428	207,885	62,507	189,869	58,641

*Assumes earnings on withdrawals are subject to a state tax rate of 5%.

**Assumes a state income tax deduction of $2,250 and $1,000, respectively, for the 18- and 8-year time frames each year based on a $5,000 annual investment to the in-state 529 Plan. These tax savings are assumed to be reinvested in the plan.

The hypothetical example shows the potential after-tax assets accumulated for college using various college investment strategies and is not intended to represent the returns of any specific investment. The analysis is based on a $5,000 annual investment in a large-cap growth fund with an assumed annualized pretax return of 8%. The analysis also assumes a 25% federal income tax rate for the parent and 10% for the child (age 14 or older), and a state tax rate of 5%. Dividends and long-term capital gains are taxed at 15% for parents and 5% for the child. Earnings in the out-of-state 529 plan are exempt from federal taxation, but are taxed at the state level. No state income tax deduction on contributions applies. Earnings in the in-state 529 plans are exempt from federal and state taxation. This example also assumes an additional administrative fee of .30% for the 529 plans. Under an UGMA/UTMA, if the child is under age 14, the first $750 of unearned income is free of tax, and the next $750 is taxed at the child's rate. Amounts over $1,500 are taxed at the parents' marginal tax rate until the child turns 14. After that, all unearned income above $750 is taxed at the child's rate. Taxable accounts in the name of a parent are taxed at the parent's tax rate.

Source: T. Rowe Price Associates, Inc.

GETTING TRACTION

Tony Bogar had heard it all before. The 33-year-old grade-school teacher had heard from his parents, his grandparents, and his coworkers about how he had to start paying more attention to his personal finances.

"Heck, I was even starting to hear it from some of my students," he joked.

Bogar began reading up on the topic and soon learned that he was nowhere near ready to take command of his long-term financial needs because he hadn't built any foundation to work from.

"I'd read where financial experts said you need 70 percent to 80 percent of your preretirement income to live comfortably once you quit working," he says. "I recalled thinking that if I retired like I planned to at age 55, I could still easily live into my 90s, like many members of my family have. But could I afford to?"

Bogar went right to work building a computer spreadsheet detailing where he was financially, how much he was spending and how much he was bringing in, and how much he estimated he needed to live on in retirement.

"I found one of those 'retirement calculators' on the Web and plugged all my information in. I made sure that I included my wife's salary and the projected cost of sending my two kids to college and the projected cost of my daughter's wedding to her boyfriend, Cooper. It really opened my eyes to the work that was ahead of me."

Still, Bogar was glad he finally had a blueprint to work from for planning his family's financial future. "It's funny," he says. "I always took financial planning for granted. But once I found out that I was the best person available to make sure I met my financial needs, well, the rest was easy. I knew right then that I had to take control because, despite what the big brokerage and mutual fund firms say, nobody else was going to know my financial picture as well as I would."

CHAPTER REVIEW

- It's entirely plausible—indeed advisable—to launch a savings program even as you pay your student loans.
- Max out on your 401(k) plan and be a millionaire by 55.
- Check out index funds and see why they're so popular among beginning investors.
- If you're starting a family, eliminate or reduce your children's college loan debt by using a 529 plan.

9

WEB SAVVY—MUST-HAVE RESOURCES FOR THE STUDENT LOAN SET

When all is said and done, the best student loan repayment strategy is getting good information and acting on it. Pretty simple, right? Hopefully, that's exactly what you've learned so far from this book. Getting the right information and knowing what to do with it is what I always figured this book should be about.

Still, it's only one book and, despite my best intentions, I can't cover everything. Thus, the need for a chapter that goes above and beyond the information already provided in these pages.

I truly believe that information is the most powerful weapon a student loan borrower has in his or her arsenal (okay, and the discipline to do something with that information, too). It's no secret that information is the key to success in any endeavor. However you can get information doesn't matter as much as simply getting that information.

I recall a story in Robert Caro's second installment of his excellent biography on former President Lyndon Johnson, *Master of the Senate.* Caro cites Johnson's penchant, as a freshman senator, for soaking up as much information as he could. Johnson would go to the bathroom ten times a day and never use the private bathroom in his Senate office. Instead, he made the walk to the Senate chamber's main bathroom, just off the Senate floor, so that he could "accidentally" bump into other senators and get them talking. He did this to make contacts and to pick up information. Meaningful information.

After all, there are varying degrees of information. Some information is useful and some is not. Albert Einstein once dismissed a questioner who asked how many feet were in a mile. "I don't know," Einstein answered. "Why should I fill my head with things like that when I could look them up in a reference book in two minutes?"

Here, in Chapter 9, I want to provide you with additional information on student loans that amplifies much of the material covered in this book. Of course, I am biased, and I think this book is an excellent resource on the subject matter. But you'd be crazy not to avail yourself of additional useful information on student loan debt that is so pervasive and so easily accessible, especially on the Internet.

My father always maintained that the key to any life plan is information—and that you could never get too much. Let's put that idea into action right now.

OVERALL STUDENT LOAN REPAYMENT RESOURCES

There is a wealth of good, broad-based resources for student loan debt management on the Web. The following sites were some of the best I visited while researching this book:

The U.S. Department of Education (http://www.ed.gov). The Granddaddy of them all, the U.S. Department of Education Web site is a great "go-to" place for all things student loan. As the site says, the Department of Education provides more than $67 billion in student loans (2002 average estimate). That's about 70 percent of all U.S. student loans.

I particularly like the department's student loan repayment site—http://studentaid.ed.gov/PORTALSWebApp/students/english/index.jsp.

It offers an educational section called "Find Aid" at http://www.ed.gov/finaid/landing.jhtml?src=rt. There you'll find loads of data and information on financial aid such as loans, grants, and work study; how they work; and the best strategies to repay them.

The department's site also boasts a library section at http://www.ifap.ed.gov/IFAPWebApp/index.jsp. It provides a nice glimpse on how loans are approved, administered, and managed.

Nellie Mae (https://loanlink.nelliemae.com/edvisor/?rf=http://www.nelliemae.com/managingmoney/;SCR=2). Another great site that covers the student loan debt issue like a blanket, from the lending institution Nellie Mae. The site likens the student loan process to climbing a mountain, and offers a step-by-step guideline for conquering that mountain, with sections called "Base Camp" and "Lacing Up Your Hiking Boots." Nice touch and very user-friendly.

Student College Loan.com (http://www.studentcollegeloan.com/links.html). A thorough site that is rich with information, if not as surefootedly structured as the Department of Education and Nellie Mae sites. What I really like is its story archives on dealing with student loan debt. Everything from "Calculating the Cost of College" to "Loosening Student Loan Debt" to "Keeping a Good Credit History" is included in the site's robust archival section. There are also links to loan consolidators and credit repair firms, although you really have to be careful before signing on to such services. A good vetting process is advised.

Here are some other good student loan debt management Web sites I like:

- **http://www.finaid.org.** Provides information about financial aid options for medical students, links to other Web sites, and a list of resources.
- **http://www.aamc.org.** A great site for medical students and medical school graduates. Great section on financial aid.
- **http://www.fastweb.com.** Nice section on finding scholarships, if you're thinking of going back to school, or are still there.
- **http://www.ed.gov/finaid.html.** From the U.S. Department of Education again. Just loads of information on loan and financial aid programs. You can also download free forms, such as the Free Application for Federal Student Aid (FAFSA).

STUDENT LOAN GOVERNMENT PUBLICATIONS

There are also plenty of publications and white papers on paying off student loans on the Web. Again, some of the best are located on the sites previously mentioned. But here are a few I really like, to save you the time of looking for them:

Federal Student Aid's *Repaying Your Student Loan Debt (http://studentaid.ed.gov/students/publications/repaying_loans/2003_2004/english/index.htm).* The whole enchilada from the FSA's point of view on student loan repayment strategies. Not as much on the basics as I'd like—things such as factoring in credit and budgeting issues aren't emphasized—but good stuff on the actual, physical process of paying back your loans. Plenty of tips on that process, too.

U.S. Department of Education's *Guide to Defaulted Student Loans (http://www.ed.gov/offices/OSFAP/DCS/index.html).* I know, there's that site again. But the department really hits the nail on the head with this handy e-booklet regarding defaulted student loans: what they mean, what your options are, and what to do.

Nellie Mae (http://www.nelliemae.com/managingmoney/bro chures.html). This is basically the "Brochures" section of the Nellie Mae Web site, but it's well worth a visit. It is chock-full of handy guides like *Steps to Success* (preparing for college costs), *On Course for Repayment* (starting the repayment process), and the *Guide to Federal PLUS Loans* (getting government student loans and then paying them back).

Note: All of Nellie Mae's student loan brochures are available in hard copy by e-mailing http://loancounselors@nelliemae.com.

PAYING YOUR STUDENT LOANS ONLINE

Want to pay your student loans automatically? As I've mentioned previously, paying electronically is great—it promotes regular payments, and many lenders will even cut your loan interest rate liability if you pay online.

If you have a government student loan, check out:

Federal Student Aid (http://studentaid.ed.gov/PORTALSWebApp/ students/english/edebit.jsp?tab=repaying). The site offers advice on electronic payment and debiting services and how the process works.

DIFFICULTY REPAYING YOUR STUDENT LOANS?

Having trouble paying off your loans? A good resource for that issue can be found at:

Federal Student Aid (http://studentaid.ed.gov/PORTALSWebApp/ students/english/difficulty.jsp?tab=repaying). Here you'll find good advice on dealing with loan troubles, with particularly strong sections on deferment and forbearance. You can also reach the FAS via its Direct Loan Servicing Center at http://www.dl.ed.gov or by calling 800-848-0979 or 315-738-6634.

LOAN DISCHARGE AND CANCELLATION

A complete, bookend-to-bookend site on how to cancel a student loan (if you are eligible) comes also from the good people at Federal Student Aid at:

Federal Student Aid (http://studentaid.ed.gov/PORTALSWeb App/students/english/discharges.jsp?tab=repaying). Here you'll find plenty of useful information on loan discharges and cancellations—the criteria you have to meet to cancel your loans, and unique, case-by-case issues such as if your school closed before you graduated or if you filed for bankruptcy.

WHERE TO FIND *YOUR* STUDENT LOAN INFORMATION

Before you begin any serious loan repayment campaign, you have to know who holds your loan and who you are dealing with. Usually that means contacting your lender directly (any invoice or statement from them will include a phone number or Web site). But if you still can't locate them, try the following avenues:

National Student Loan Data System (NSLDS). The NSLDS bills itself as the central location for all your federal student loan and Pell Grant information needs. Reach them by phone at 800-4-FED-AID or visit http://www.nslds.ed.gov and click "Financial Aid Review." You'll need a federal PIN to access your loan data. If you forgot your PIN, visit http://pin.ed.gov/request.htm to get a new one.

National Student Clearinghouse—Loan Locator. Strictly for participating Federal Family Education Loan Program (FFELP) guarantors. Visit the Clearinghouse at http://studentclearing house.org/secure_area/loan_locator.asp. You can also access the Clearinghouse via ElmNet (a loan inquiry service) at http://www .elmnet.elmproduction.com. Enter your Social Security number and date of birth to access your records at each site.

You can also access your loan information via the three major U.S. credit bureaus:

Equifax
P.O. Box 740241
Atlanta, GA 30374-0241
http://www.equifax.com
800-685-1111

Experian
P.O. Box 2002
Allen, TX 75013
http://www.experian.com
888-397-3742

TransUnion
2 Baldwin Place
P.O. Box 1000
Chester, PA 19022
http://www.tuc.com
800-888-4213

INFORMATION ON DIFFERENT TYPES OF STUDENT LOANS

There are loads of Web sites—from banks, lending institutions, government agencies, and the like—on the various types of student loans. Just save yourself the trouble of looking and go to the best one (in my opinion) at:

College Financial Planning (http://www.collegefinancialplanning .com/loans.htm). Everything you've ever wanted to know about the various types of student loans is on the site, including a helpful treatise on subsidized and unsubsidized loans (and what they mean to you and your loan situation). A good pros and cons section is located there, too.

STUDENT LOAN DEBT CONSOLIDATION PROGRAMS

I swear, after researching this book I now believe that debt consolidation Web sites have overtaken diet, porn, and home equity mortgage sites as the most pervasive type of site on the entire World Wide Web. So much to choose from and so much to look out for, ethics-wise.

But, having reviewed seemingly millions of them, here are the ones I think work best if you're interested in more information on consolidating your student loan or loans:

Student Loan Consolidation Center (SLCC) (http://ads.247wsr .com/). Student Loan Consolidation Center and private education loan consolidation.

Direct Consolidation Loans (http://loanconsolidation.ed.gov/). U.S. Department of Education Web site that provides information to borrowers, schools, and loan holders. You can also apply online to consolidate your student loans.

Guide to Defaulted Student Loans (http://www.ed.gov/). Billed as a "comprehensive guide for student loan borrowers with defaulted student loans." I read through the site and it seems to deliver as advertised. But, then again, it is from the U.S. Department of Education, so it better be thorough.

FinancialAid.com (http://www.financialaid.com/). Good deals on consolidated loans, although when I read through this site in late 2003, interest rates were still relatively low.

Lending Tree (http://www.lendingtree.com). You've seen the commercials, now see the real thing.

Sallie Mae (http://www.salliemae.com). Another government-sponsored lending agency, Sallie Mae has developed a great reputation over the years as an ethical, viable lending option for students. Financial services company offers students loans and financial aid to students and their parents. If I were applying for a consolidated student loan, and if I were eligible, this is the site I would visit first.

FINANCIAL AID PROGRAMS AND RESOURCES

Wired Scholar (http://www.usafunds.wiredscholar.com/usafunds/content/index.jsp). If you're looking for financial aid, you can't go wrong by visiting Wired Scholar. There is plenty of advice and tools to help you understand the admissions and financial aid processes.

MANAGING CREDIT

If you've read the entire book up until now, you know I'm big on understanding debt management and credit. That probably stems from my background working on a Wall Street bond trading desk, where credit and debt were (and are) the Holy Grail of the bond business.

At the student loan level—or really at the younger consumer level—you can find some good background information on credit and debt at the following sites:

Institute for Consumer Financial Education (http://www.icfe.info). The ICFE is nonprofit with a Web site full of credit and budgeting tips. It even has a nice section on teaching children about money. Offers a good do-it-yourself credit repair kit, too.

Nellie Mae (http://www.nelliemae.com/managingmoney/cc_tips .html). Nellie Mae, again, this time with a good site on credit card tips for younger Americans, particularly college students.

FINDING A STUDENT LOAN OMBUDSMAN

I covered this topic in the book, and reiterate that a college loan ombudsman (most schools have them) can be a real ally for you in your student loan repayment campaign.

Here is a list of the state-by-state ombudsmen, along with contact information, available (through 2003):

Colorado Student Loan Program (CSLP)
999 18th Street, Suite 425
Denver, CO 80202
Phone: 303-305-3274
Fax: 303-305-3515

Connecticut Student Loan Foundation (CSLF)
P.O. Box 1009
Rocky Hill, CT 06067
Phone: 800-237-9721, ext. 224
Fax: 860-257-1743

EDFUND
P.O. Box 419045
Rancho Cordova, CA 95741-9045
Phone: 916-526-8024
Fax: 916-526-8518

Education Assistance Corporation (EAC)
115 First Avenue S.W.
Aberdeen, SD 57401
Phone: 800-592-1802, ext. 4301

Educational Credit Management Corporation (ECMC)
P.O. Box 64909
St. Paul, MN 55164-0909
Phone: 651-325-3015
Fax: 651-325-3195

Georgia Higher Education Assistance Corporation (GHEAC)
2082 East Exchange Place
Tucker, GA 30084
Phone: 800-776-6878, ext. 9137
Fax: 770-724-9131

Illinois Student Assistance Commission (ISAC)
1755 Lake Cook Road
Deerfield, IL 60015
Phone: 800-899-4722, ext. 2708
Fax: 847-831-8549

Iowa College Student Aid Commission (ICSAC)
200 10th Street, 4th Floor
Des Moines, IA 50309

Kentucky Higher Education Assistance Authority (KIHEAA)
P.O. Box 79
Frankfort, KY 40601
Phone: 800-928-8926, ext. 7278
Fax: 502-696-7305

Missouri Department of Higher Education/Missouri Student Loan Group Information Center
3515 Amazonas Drive
Jefferson City, MO 65109-5717
Phone: 800-473-6757, option 1

National Student Loan Program (NSLP)
1300 O Street
Lincoln, NE 68508
Phone: 800-735-8778
Fax: 402-479-6762

New Hampshire Higher Education Assistance Foundation (NHHEAF)
P.O. Box 2087
Concord, NH 03302-2087
Phone: 800-525-2577, ext. 120

New Jersey Higher Education Student Assistance Authority (HESAA)
P.O. Box 540
Trenton, NJ 08625
Phone: 609-588-3351

New York State Higher Education Services Corporation (NYSHESC)
99 Washington Avenue
Albany, New York 12255
Phone: 518-408-0004

North Carolina State Education Assistance Authority (NCSEAA)
P.O. Box 14002
Research Triangle Park, NC 27709-4002
Phone: 919-248-4626 or 800-700-1775, ext. 626

Northwest Education Loan Association (NELA)
190 Queen Anne Avenue N., Suite 300
Seattle, WA 98109
Phone: 800-562-3001, ext. 5453

Rhode Island Higher Education Assistance Authority (RIHEAA)
560 Jefferson Boulevard
Warwick, RI 02886
Phone: 401-736-1162

South Carolina Student Loan Corporation (SCSLC)
P.O. Box 21487
Columbia, SC 29221
Phone: 803-612-5030
Fax: 803-772-9410

Student Loan Guaranty Foundation of Arkansas (SLGFA)
219 South Victory Street
Little Rock, AR 72201
Phone: 800-622-3446, ext. 661

Student Loans of North Dakota
P.O. Box 5524
Bismarck, ND 58506-5524

Texas Guaranteed (TG)
P.O. Box 201725
Austin, Texas 78720-1725
Phone: 800-252-9743, ext. 4502

United Student Aid Funds, Inc. (USA Funds)
P.O. Box 6028, MC 8516
Indianapolis, IN 46206-6028
Phone: 866-329-7673, ext. 1260

Vermont Student Assistance Commission (VSAC)
P.O. Box 2000
Winooski, VT 05404
Phone: 800-642-3177, ext. 350
Fax: 800-654-3765

STUDENT LOAN AND DEBT CALCULATORS

Let's end the chapter with a rundown of some of the best financial calculators on the Web. They provide quick and easy ways to figure out loan payments, liabilities, and timetables.

Mapping Your Future (http://www.mapping-your-future.org/features /budgetcalc.htm).

Ivillage.com (http://www.ivillage.com/money/life_stage/startingout/ articles/0,10509,188832_98792,00.html.

The National Institution for Consumer Education (http://www .nice.emich.edu/IdentityTheft).

HAPPY HUNTING

Look, I'm not going to insult your intelligence by saying these resources encompass the best information you're going to find on student loan debt on the Internet. Not by a long shot.

But between this book, and the information I've given you previously, you should be well equipped to tackle not only your student loan debt challenges, but your overall debt management challenges as well.

After all, despite what Madison Avenue tells you, image isn't everything. When it comes to college debts, information is.

10

FIFTY-PLUS STUDENT LOAN DEBT TIPS YOU CAN TAKE TO THE BANK

Call this the "value chapter." I've written ten or so how-to books on financial matters, and I love to end them this way—with valuable tips on how to solve the problems you set out to solve. With your student loans, that sure is a lot of ground to cover.

I know, you have to be careful about giving advice. Remember Socrates, the Greek philosopher? He ran around giving everyone advice and they wound up poisoning him. But I'm confident that you'll keep me around no matter what, if only to flog me later for dishing out a bad tidbit or two on student loan management. But I think the good will easily outweigh the bad. At least it better.

Let's start with some tips on good money management and then roll into student loan tips.

MONEY MANAGEMENT TIPS

The key to good money management skills is to use just plain old common sense. Here are more than 50 tips to help you do just that:

1. **Have a plan.** During my senior year in college, when my campaign for my first professional job kicked off, my father told me only one thing: "Have a plan." Wise words indeed. Use the information in this book to develop a solid plan for building your own student loan repayment campaign and managing it effectively. Decide early on your budget, your income estimates, and how much you can afford to pay.

2. **Set goals.** Any good marksman will tell you the key to hitting a target is having a target. Having something to aim at, to work toward, gives you the framework for a successful student loan repayment plan.

3. **Stick with your plan.** Things aren't always going to go the way you want them to. When things go awry, the only way you'll know is by monitoring your loan payment campaign on a regular basis, once or twice a month. The more your pay and the more frequently you pay, the more you'll enjoy going online or checking your loan statements to see how much progress you're making in paying off your loan.

4. **Include your spouse or partner in your loan payment plan.** Nobody likes surprises so keep your loved ones apprised of your student loan payment activities. Talk about goals and budgets and things that might come up to thwart your payment plans, like loss of a job or an expanded household expense situation. Bonus: By keeping your loved one informed, you'll have a good sounding board to bounce ideas and strategies off of. Plus, he or she can prove to be a real ally if your lender comes back someday and says

you didn't pay your loans. A spouse or a family member's testimony that you did pay weighs heavily in those situations.

5. Have patience. There's no formula I know of, outside of a winning Powerball ticket, to create financial security overnight. In this instance, the best way to gain that financial security is to pay off your student loan debt and get that good credit rating you need. Just relax, monitor your payments, and watch your debt burden subside and your attractiveness to creditors rise.

6. Do your homework. Read your loan statements, check your loan obligations, watch your spending, and keep this book handy. In short, do anything you can to bone up on your student loans and thus get them paid off faster.

7. No "impulse" buying. The worst thing you can do to set your student loan payment momentum back is to overspend—especially on things you don't need. Check those impulses and keep thinking how easier it will be to buy things that matter—a new home for your family and new furnishings for that home with your student loan debt paid off.

8. Charge only if you *have* to—and only if you can afford to pay right away. Put the charge card away unless you really need it. One strategy I employ is to use my credit card only if I have money in my bank account to cover it. The thing with charge card abuse is that you can never really count on future income—only future expenses. So leave your credit card in a desk drawer somewhere until your loans are paid off. And if you do have a credit card maxed out or canceled, don't open a new one until the old card is paid off.

9. Make a list. This is a good budgeting exercise designed to let you know where you stand on an income or an outflow basis. Begin by jotting down your incoming assets, for example, paychecks, employee bonuses, or investments (if you have any), and your expenses (that's likely a longer list). Itemize everything and begin tracking each dollar that leaves your home and enters it. Do this on a monthly basis and you'll soon know where you stand financially.

10. **Separate good debt from bad debt.** Get rid of those "bad debt" high-interest credit card debts first, before you pay off your student loan debt (which invariably will have lower interest rates attached). Also, weigh the pros and cons of paying off your debt versus investing in the stock market. Earlier in the book I maintained that you could do both—pay down your school debt while you invest in a 401(k) or other tax-advantaged retirement plan. And you can. But if you have a preference for investing in the markets, and you can make the 10 percent or so in annual investment returns you'll need to stay well ahead of inflation, investing while paying the debt minimum on your school loan is certainly an option.

11. **Be wary of preapproved credit cards.** Who hasn't opened up his or her mailbox to find a preapproved credit card offer or two? A cynic might say that whole forests have been toppled for the sole reason of getting your signature on a shiny new credit card. Nice line. But the best way to keep credit card debt down is by not using a credit card. If you do receive a preapproved card that intrigues you, at least know what you're getting into before signing on the bottom line. The keys to look for?

- Know what interest you're paying.
- Realize that your interest rates can vary (and climb upward).
- Understand the penalty of paying your credit card bill late (some cards will immediately raise your interest rate from the introductory teaser rate to the regular rate if you're late just one time).
- Whatever you do, don't pay any fees. You're the customer— make them compete for *your* business.

12. Know what to do if you have a credit card and lose it. We all know the feeling. Back home after a night out on the town, or returning from a day at the beach, you reach into your back pocket or your purse for your wallet and come up empty. Cue the sinking feeling in your belly. If you do lose your credit card, make sure to take the following steps:

- **Report your card loss to your credit card company.** Because most credit card fraud occurs within the first 48 hours of your card being lost, contact your credit card company right away. The sooner you report the loss, the less the damage can be done to your credit card liability.
- **Call the cops.** Credit card fraud is a criminal offense. If a card thief tries to use your card after it's been reported stolen, employees of most large retail stores are trained to contact the police, or have their manager do it for them behind the scenes. That way, not only is the thief caught, any fraudulent use of your card will come to a swift end.
- **Start a paper trail.** Sure it's inconvenient. But if you record the time and date you place calls to issuers, as well as the first and last names of the service representative who assists you and any other relevant information, this could save you big-time aggravation down the road. To help prevent the theft of your credit card and ATM cards down the road, make sure your card is signed on the signature panel as soon as you receive it. Also, protect your cards as if they were cash. Don't leave them unattended anywhere, such as in a car, bar, nightclub, or on the beach. With ATM cards, never write down your PIN—memorize it, instead.
- **Make a record of your credit card account numbers.** Also include telephone numbers for reporting lost or stolen cards.
- **Lastly, open your credit card bill as soon as it arrives.** Match your receipts with the transactions listed in your statement. Verify that the total amount for each transaction matches the receipt you signed. Reconcile the account like

a checkbook to be certain that your card has not been used without your knowledge.

13. **Know your credit rating.** Make sure you regularly check your credit reports for information regarding your credit rating. Do this at least on a semiannual basis. Your credit rating is your barometer of financial health so you always want to know where you stand. Remember, your credit rating is how lenders think of you.

14. **Order a free credit report** By law, the credit agencies have to, once a year, make your credit report available to you free of charge. Take advantage of that and get your credit report free from the three major credit bureaus.

15. **Know your credit score.** Credit bureaus award scores to those individuals who have taken student loans—or any loans or credit actions—by grading how fast they pay those debts back. Your credit bureau can tell you your credit score—the measurement that lenders and creditors use when deciding whether or not to extend you credit. They do so by awarding points to you, based on your ability to pay off your debts. Those points help creditors evaluate how creditworthy you are, that is, how likely you will repay a loan and make the payments when due.

16. **Know how to fix bad credit.** The best way to fix bad credit is to pay your debts on time. But if things have gotten away from you financially, make sure to contact your creditors immediately and let them know you intend to pay your debt obligations. If you don't, they'll assume the worst and start treating you like a deadbeat, with collection agencies calling and nasty notes arriving in the mail. Be up front and chances are you can work something out.

17. **Keep your bills manageable.** Don't get in over your head; but if you do, stop and take corrective action. By and large, your

monthly debt payments should not exceed 10 percent to 15 percent of your take-home pay each month.

18. Keep your ATM trips to a minimum. It's easy to get in the habit of hitting the ATM machine every time your wallet is empty. Not only do you keep siphoning cash out of your bank account (and out of your student loan payments) but you could also be charged up to $2 per transaction by the bank for the privilege. Resist that urge by creating a budget with spending limits, where you visit the ATM at most once a week.

19. When out on the town with your buddies, don't pay the bill with your credit card. One of the worst things you can do to your budget is to pay the dinner tab while out with your friends and then accept cash from them as payment. All you're doing is potentially adding up to 20 percent extra on top of the dinner bill. That's the interest on the credit card if you don't pay your monthly bill on time.

20. Get a roommate. If you're just out of school and feeling a financial squeeze and you don't want to move in with Mom and Dad (can't blame you there), get a roommate to move in with you. Besides cutting your rent in half, you can cut living expenses like utility bills in half, too.

21. Don't buy a car—use public transportation. A new car may seem all bright and shiny, but it loses 40 percent of its value when you drive it off the lot and it can sap your bank account in maintenance. Cars are "moving money pits." According to Intelli-Choice.com, a car purchased in 1998 costs $37,322 to own over five years. That includes depreciation, gas and oil, financing, average maintenance, repairs, government registration fees, and insurance. Depreciation (including car payments) is the big-ticket item, comprising 36 percent of the true cost; insurance and financing, at 24 percent and 15 percent, respectively, follow. Fees and, somewhat surprisingly, repairs are the lowest contributors to a car's true cost, at 3 percent and 2.5 percent, respectively. Better to use public transportation and keep that money where it belongs—working to pay off your student loan debt.

22. If you have to buy a big-ticket item, at least use manufacturers' rebates. Buying a big-screen television or a new washer and dryer may have its merits, but it won't help you pay off your debts any faster. But, if you insist, at least use manufacturers' rebates when you do. A few tips:

- Any rebate deal will require you to buy the product first before getting a rebate—that's why they call them rebates.
- After you purchase the product, fill out all the paperwork and submit it as soon as possible. Normally, the manufacturer requires this information be mailed within 15 days of purchase. Unless otherwise stated, rebates are paid by check. However, some rebates, like online deals at a Web flower shop or book dealer, will credit the credit card account used when signing up for the service. On average, you'll receive a check within eight to ten weeks. Rebates that have a high volume response sometimes take longer.
- Make sure you hang on to your receipt because many manufacturers demand the original sales receipt before paying out your rebate. Tip: Make a photocopy to keep for your records. (If you're buying a number of items at one time, and one or more have offer rebates, you might want to ask for separate sales receipts for the rebate items.)
- Also jot down the name and address of the manufacturer's rebate address, along with the brand name, model number, and any other key product data. Many manufacturers use outside "fulfillment" houses to process rebates, so the rebate address may not be the address of the manufacturer.
- If you have a beef with the manufacturer, don't contact the fulfillment house, go right to the manufacturer and state your case.

- Don't deep-six the product packaging until your rebate check is in hand. The packaging could include data the manufacturer requires (nobody ever said rebates would be easy), including uniform product code (UPC) symbols, a special logo, or a box top.

Before you send the rebate in, make sure you:

- Sign all areas of the form requiring a signature and write clearly so the rebate company won't have to obtain more information.
- Read all rebate terms and make sure you understand them. It is important that you read the guidelines of the rebate carefully and submit the rebate according to those guidelines.
- Make a copy of any rebate form you submit and file it in a safe place. You may be asked to resend it in case your information is not clear. Also, some manufacturers require proof of purchase for warranty service.
- Print out any rebate forms associated with a product immediately upon ordering. This way you'll have the form available when you wish to redeem the rebate.
- Make copies of all sales receipts, labels, UPCs, and any correspondence that you had with the manufacturer, store, or clearinghouse that handles rebates.
- Keep records of when you mailed your rebate packet and who you talked to if you made follow-up calls.

23. Use e-mail instead of making long distance phone calls. Sounds simple, right? But it works. Instead of spending $22 calling your old buddies on the phone after a night out at the bars, send an e-mail for cents on the dollar.

24. Use EDWISE (www.edwise.org). This is a cool online financial planning Web site geared specifically toward college and postcollege individuals looking for help in jelling their financial lifestyles. It offers plenty of tutorials and calculators and other information to help you plan your postgraduate years from a financial point of view.

25. Use the *Occupational Outlook Handbook* (www.bls.gov/oco home.htm). The handbook is a great tool for figuring out how much you might make in a job in your chosen profession. This comes in handy when you're plotting out your financial budget. The handbook comes complete with estimated student loan payments (monthly) and estimated income worksheets to help you balance everything out. It's well worth the money.

26. Final advice on financial lifestyle management. When you create your lifestyle budget, always aim lower in expenses and higher on the savings end. Eliminate as many cushy, noncritical items as you can and keep your entertainment expenses as low as possible. Don't worry, you'll be over such lifestyle sacrifices before you know it, and on to bigger and better things once your student loan is paid off.

STUDENT LOAN REPAYMENT TIPS

I've advocated paying your student loans debts off quickly and efficiently. Time to back that sentiment up with some more helpful tips:

26. Get organized. Gather your student loan documents and know what your financial obligations are and how much money you owe. Have this information at your fingertips, ideally in a file in your home. It's okay to put this information online, but keep hard copy files, too. Those are the ones you might have to show a lender or a credit counselor if troubles arise.

Make sure to save:

- Loan applications, promissory notes, disbursement and disclosure statements, and loan transfer notices
- Copies of all correspondence with your lender and your school's financial aid office
- Current addresses and telephone numbers of your lender
- The names and numbers (including e-mail addresses) of lending institution contacts and the date and time of the conversations

28. Know who your lender is. Don't laugh, many people don't. Start with the information I gave you in Chapter 8 and contact:

- **National Student Loan Data System (NSLDS).** Go to http://www.nslds.ed.gov and click on "Financial Aid Review." You'll need a federal PIN to access your loan data. If you forgot your PIN, visit http://pin.ed.gov/request.htm to get a new one.
- **National Student Clearinghouse—Loan Locator (http://www.studentclearinghouse.org/secure_area/loan_locator.asp.).** If that doesn't work, contact your school or former school's bursar's or financial aid office. Have your name and Social Security number ready.

29. Know what the phrase *Six months and 45 days* means. That's usually the date after you graduate or leave school when your government student loan payments are expected to kick in. Don't wait for that date to hit you upside the head. Have your first payment ready. Better yet, start putting money aside sooner than that if you can. Prepaying is a student loan borrower's best friend.

30. Know your repayment options. We went over this in great detail in Chapter 3.

- A fixed repayment plan means just that—it's a standardized, fixed payment every month.
- A graduated repayment plan allows you to pay as your income increases.
- An income-contingent payment plan allows you to declare some type of financial hardship and pay what you can on your student loans.

31. Know what a *deferment* means. With a deferment, your lender okays your delaying the repayment of the principal of your loan for a predetermined period of time.

Interest on the loan may or may not accrue, depending on the type of loan you have. With Perkins or Stafford loans, no interest accrues during the deferment period, because the federal government pays the interest. For unsubsidized loans or private loans, interest continues to accrue throughout the deferment period.

Note that you may be able to take a break on interest payments on any type of loan during a deferment by "capitalizing" the loan. That means adding the existing interest onto the loan principal and rolling it into one big ball of financial obligations for you. Paying interest on interest is no way to go through life.

32. Know what *forbearance* means. Forbearance is a mechanism designed to help if you need to either temporarily lower or postpone your student loan payments. Forbearance is really for those folks who want to pay their loans but can't, but were unable to get a deferment on their loans. The application process isn't as onerous as the one for deferments, and the bureaucratic headaches that always seem to accompany deferments and loan discharges aren't as prevalent with a forbearance. Note, though, that it is (again) completely up to the lending institution to determine whether you are awarded forbearance.

If you are approved, be prepared to continue paying interest on your loan. If you can't, the lender will simply add it to the ongoing loan bill and it will cost you even more money.

FIGURE 10.1 *Total Amount Paid on a Loan of $10,000 at an Interest Rate of 8.25 Percent*

Loan Amount:	$10,000
Interest Rate:	8.25%
Repayment Period:	10 years
Number of Payments:	120
Each Payment:	$122.65
Total Amount Repaid:	$14,718

33. Know the meaning of the words *principal* and *interest*. Principal is the amount of money you borrowed on your loan. Of course you have to pay that back. But you also have to pay the interest back. Interest is the additional amount that you pay to the lender for the privilege of borrowing their money. It's their profit margin.

The marriage of principal and interest is simple: when you accept a loan from a lending institution, the money you ultimately owe is more than the amount you receive because of the interest (see Figure 10.1 for an example).

34. Pay more on your monthly bill—and save interest. If you can manage to send a few extra bucks every month, go ahead and pay more than you owe (per your minimum loan balance). By doing so, you save big bucks on your overall interest payments. On a loan at 8 percent interest, paying an additional $50 a month—$600 over the course of the first year—leads to $1,300 in savings on your loan payment principal over the first nine years of your loan.

35. Minimize the chance of default by your good "graces." Use your student loan's grace period to save up money for your student loan payments. As I said in Chapter 5, the trick here is to forget that it's a "grace" period. Treat it as a "loan payment" period.

36. Keep your lender in the loop. Don't hesitate to contact your lending institution as soon as you begin to have problems handling your student loan. They can help with payment plans and some new financing options. If you can't pay—and don't say—then you're begging for a default situation.

37. Go to Uncle Sam for help on avoiding default. Got a default loan? The U.S. Department of Education Debt Collection Service can help. It publishes a guide called *Guide to Defaulted Student Loans* to help students repay their defaulted student loans. It includes information about:

- Repaying a defaulted student loan
- Loan consolidation
- Loan cancellation and discharge

Call 800-4-FED-AID [800-433-3243] or 800-621-3115 for a copy.

38. Tax rule—in your favor. Take full advantage of student loan IRS rules. You may easily qualify for any federal tax breaks such as the Hope or Lifetime Learning tax credit. A bonus: You may be able to deduct your student loan interest payments on your tax return.

39. Take a (financial) break. If you just graduated from college and want to move on up to graduate school—but money is an issue—take a break. Go to work and get some real-world experience in your field, and accumulate some more money to pay off those loans, both undergraduate and future graduate. That's the best of both worlds—great experience in your field and some cash to square your loan obligations away.

40. Borrow from Mom and Dad if you have to. Borrowing money from a family member is a great way to alleviate the hefty interest payments you have to make on your student loan. You'll get lower interest rates (if any) unless you're related to Ebenezer Scrooge. But make sure you put everything in writing—it is family, after all.

41. Family values, part II. I've said this before in the book, but it bears repeating. If you get a nice check from Uncle Phil or Aunt Gladys after you graduated, there is no rule that says you have to spend it on Lasik eye surgery or a new hot tub. Instead, use "free" money to pay off your student loan debt early—and reap the financial dividends later on after your loan is paid off.

42. Make money while you're still in school. If you're in graduate school or undergraduate school, consider a business internship that pays a weekly or monthly stipend. The pay may not be much but it can help keep your debt level in check. Plus, the experience you'll earn will give you a leg up on your chosen industry.

43. Use your chosen profession to forgive your debt. If you're in a civic-minded educational program, like nursing or teaching, you may be able to use your vocation to your advantage and either diminish or "forgive" your student loan debt. Many lending institutions, on the federal level, may review your professional situation and may extend you some relief from your debt payments. Check with your school's financial aid office for help.

44. If you run into trouble, consolidate. You can potentially ease your student loan troubles by consolidating your loan. The best way for taking care of a consolidation loan is to continue making the same payments you were making before you consolidated your loan, applying the extra amount to the principal.

45. Be careful about consolidation. Don't leap into a consolidation situation without looking first. Remember that the added loan payment timetable that comes with a consolidated loan increases your total loan obligation. So only consolidate if you have to.

46. Again, Uncle Sam can help. Not sure about consolidating your student loans? The U.S. Department of Education can provide Direct Consolidation Loans and some good information on such loans. Contact them at http://www.ed.gov/directloan/ or 800-557-7392.

47. Avoid bankruptcy at all costs. Remember this: Bankruptcy is permanent and debt management is temporary. Better to try and work out your debts before resorting to that last report.

48. Always be aware that the clock is ticking. It's okay to take off a month now or then from your student loan. But keep your eye on the prize and keep making those payments. It's the surest way to financial security, sooner rather than later in life. As I've said before, you don't want to be paying off your student loans in your 40s, that's when you should be socking away money for your loved ones and for your retirement.

49. Carry your promissory note with you in your wallet or purse. This is a neat trick. By carrying your loan promissory note with you in your wallet or purse, you'll always have a vivid reminder of your serious financial obligations. That may come in handy as you pull out that Visa card to pay for that $1,200 vintage Japanese figurine for your living room.

50. Customize your monthly student loan bill. Lending institutions are only too happy to accommodate you—within reason. One way they will do so is to agree to your monthly billing date. Maybe you are paid once a month—on the 15th—and you want your student loan bill to come on the 20th. Ask your lender and chances are you'll get the invoice date you want.

51. Pay your loan off. That's it. Oh . . . one more thing.

52. Celebrate your liberation from student loan debt. Once you pay off your last student loan debt, by all means celebrate. You've cleared the way for a bright and shiny financial future and you should be congratulated for it. So, enjoy all the benefits and all the power that your new financial status provides. Heck, take a little of the money you've saved by using some of the tips in this book and taxes and buy a nice bottle of champagne for you and your friends. Open it and toast the new financial you. As you sip the bubbly, consider how far you've come in taking control of your financial life. After all, nobody has as much invested in your financial future as you do.